SPEEDPRO SERIES

HOW TO GET STARTED IN

MOTOR SPORT

Also from Veloce Publishing:

SpeedPro Series

Getting started in Motorsport by Sam Collins
How to Blueprint & Build a 4-Cylinder Engine Short Block for High Performance by Des Hammill
How to Build a V8 Engine Short Block for High Performance by Des Hammill
How to Plan and Build a Fast Road Car by Daniel Stapleton
How to Build & Modify Sportscar/Kitcar Suspension & Brakes by Des Hammill
How to Build & Modify SU Carburettors for High Performance by Des Hammill
How to Build & Power Tune Weber DCOE, DCO/SP & Dellorto DHLA Carburetors Third Edition by Des Hammill
How to Build & Power Tune Harley-Davidson Evolution Engines by Des Hammill
How to Build & Power Tune Holley Carburetors by Des Hammill
How to Build & Power Tune Distributor-type Ignition Systems by Des Hammill
How to Build, Modify & Power Tune Cylinder Heads Second Edition by Peter Burgess
How to Build Your Own Tiger Avon Sportscar by Jim Dudley
How to Choose Camshafts & Time them for Maximum Power by Des Hammill
How to Give your MGB V8 Power Updated & Revised Edition by Roger Williams
How to Improve the MGB, MGC & MGB V8 by Roger Williams
How to Improve the TR5, 250 & TR6 by Roger Williams
How to Improve the TR2, 3 & TR4 by Roger Williams
How to Modify Volkswagen Beetle Chassis, Suspension & Brakes for High Performance by James Hale
How to Modify Volkswagen Bus Suspension, Brakes & Chassis for High Performance by James Hale
How to Power Tune Mini Engines on a Small Budget by Des Hammill
How to Power Tune the BMC 998cc A-Series Engine by Des Hammill
How to Power Tune BMC/Rover 1275cc A-Series Engines by Des Hammill
How to Power Tune the MGB 4-Cylinder Engine by Peter Burgess
How to Power Tune the MG Midget & Austin-Healey Sprite Updated Edition by Daniel Stapleton
How to Power Tune Alfa Romeo Twin Cam Engines by Jim Kartalamakis
How to Power Tune Ford SOHC 'Pinto' & Sierra Cosworth DOHC Engines Updated & Revised Edition by Des Hammill
How to Power Tune Jaguar XK Engines by Des Hammill
How to Power Tune Rover V8 Engines by Des Hammill

Colour Family Album Series

Alfa Romeo by Andrea & David Sparrow
Bubblecars & Microcars by Andrea & David Sparrow
Bubblecars & Microcars, More by Andrea & David Sparrow
Citroen 2CV by Andrea & David Sparrow
Citroen DS by Andrea & David Sparrow
Custom VWs by Andrea & David Sparrow
Fiat & Abarth 500 & 600 by Andrea & David Sparrow
Lambretta by Andrea & David Sparrow
Mini & Mini Cooper by Andrea & David Sparrow
Motor Scooters by Andrea & David Sparrow
Porsche by Andrea & David Sparrow
Triumph Sportscars by Andrea & David Sparrow
Vespa by Andrea & David Sparrow
VW Beetle by Andrea & David Sparrow
VW Bus, Camper, Van & Pick-up by Andrea & David Sparrow
VW Custom Beetle by Andrea & David Sparrow

General

AC Two-litre Saloons & Buckand Sportscars by Leo Archibald
Alfa Romeo Berlinas (Saloons/Sedans) by John Tipler
Alfa Romeo Giulia Coupe GT & GTA Updated & Revised Edition by John Tipler
Anatomy of the Works Minis by Brian Moylan
Automotive A-Z, Lane's Dictionary of Automotive Terms by Keith Lane
Automotive Mascots by David Kay & Lynda Springate
Bentley Continental, Corniche and Azure, by Martin Bennett
BMW 5-Series by Marc Cranswick
BMW Z-Cars by James Taylor
British Cars, The Complete Catalogue of, 1895-1975 by Culshaw & Horrobin
British Police Cars by Nick Walker
British Trailer Caravans 1919-1959 by Andrew Jenkinson
British Trailer Caravans from 1960 by Andrew Jenkinson

Bugatti Type 40 by Barrie Price
Bugatti 46/50 Updated Edition by Barrie Price
Bugatti 57 2nd Edition - by Barrie Price
Caravanning & Trailer Tenting, the Essential Handbook by Len Archer
Chrysler 300 - America's Most Powerful Car by Robert Ackerson
Cobra - The Real Thing! by Trevor Legate
Cortina - Ford's Bestseller by Graham Robson
Daimler SP250 'Dart' by Brian Long
Datsun/Nissan 280ZX & 300ZX by Brian Long
Datsun Z - From Fairlady to 280Z by Brian Long
Dune Buggy Handbook by James Hale
Fiat & Abarth 124 Spider & Coupe by John Tipler
Fiat & Abarth 500 & 600 by Malcolm Bobbitt
Ford F100/F150 Pick-up by Robert Ackerson
Ford GT40 by Trevor Legate
Ford Model Y by Sam Roberts
Harley-Davidson, Growing up by Jean Davidson
Jaguar XJ-S, by Brian Long
Karmann-Ghia Coupe & Convertible by Malcolm Bobbitt
Land Rover, The Half-Ton Military by Mark Cook
Lea-Francis Story, The by Barrie Price
Lexus Story, The by Brian Long
Lola - The Illustrated History (1957-1977) by John Starkey
Lola - All The Sports Racing & Single-Seater Racing Cars 1978-1997 by John Starkey
Lola T70 - The Racing History & Individual Chassis Record 3rd Edition by John Starkey
Lotus 49 by Michael Oliver
Mazda MX-5/Miata 1.6 Enthusiast's Workshop Manual by Rod Grainger & Pete Shoemark
Mazda MX-5/Miata 1.8 Enthusiast's Workshop Manual by Rod Grainger & Pete Shoemark
Mazda MX-5 (& Eunos Roadster) - The World's Favourite Sportscar by Brian Long
MGA by John Price Williams
MGB & MGB GT - Expert Guide (Auto-Doc Series) by Roger Williams
Mini Cooper - The Real Thing! by John Tipler
Mitsubishi Lancer Evo by Brian Long
Motorhomes, History of, by Andrew Jenkinson
Motor Racing at Goodwood in the Sixties by Tony Gardiner
MR2 - Toyota's Mid-engined Sports Car by Brian Long
Porsche 356 by Brian Long
Porsche 911 1964-1971 by Brian Long
Porsche 911R, RS & RSR, 4th Ed. by John Starkey
Porsche 914 & 914-6 by Brian Long
Porsche 924 by Brian Long
Porsche 944 by Brian Long
Rolls-Royce Silver Shadow/Bentley T Series Corniche & Camargue Updated Edition by Malcolm Bobbitt
Rolls-Royce Silver Spirit, Silver Spur & Bentley Mulsanne by Malcolm Bobbitt
Rolls-Royce Silver Wraith, Dawn & Cloud/Bentley MkVI, R & S Series by Martyn Nutland
RX-7 - Mazda's Rotary Engine Sportscar by Brian Long
Singer Story: Cars, Commercial Vehicles, Bicycles & Motorcycles by Kevin Atkinson
Taxi! The Story of the 'London' Taxicab by Malcolm Bobbitt
Triumph Motorcycles & the Meriden Factory by Hughie Hancox
Triumph Tiger Cub Bible by Mike Estall
Triumph Trophy Bible by Harry Woolridge
Triumph TR2/3/3A, How to Restore, by Roger Williams
Triumph TR4/4A, How to Restore, by Roger Williams
Triumph TR5/250 & 6, How to Restore, by Roger Williams
Triumph TR6 by William Kimberley
Turner's Triumphs, Edward Turner & his Triumph Motorcycles by Jeff Clew
Velocette Motorcycles - MSS to Thruxton by Rod Burris
Volkswagens of the World by Simon Glen
VW Beetle Cabriolet by Malcolm Bobbitt
VW Beetle - The Car of the 20th Century by Richard Copping
VW Bus, Camper, Van, Pickup by Malcolm Bobbitt
Works Rally Mechanic by Brian Moylan

First published in 2003 by Veloce Publishing Ltd., 33 Trinity Street, Dorchester DT1 1TT, England.
Fax 01305 268864/e-mail info@veloce.co.uk/web www.veloce.co.uk or www.velocebooks.com
ISBN 1-903706-70-X/UPC 36847-00270-1

Readers with ideas for automotive books, or books on other transport or related hobby subjects, are invited to write to the editorial director of Veloce Publishing Ltd. at the above address.

British Library Cataloguing in Publication Data -
A catalogue record for this book is available from the British Library.

Typesetting (Soutane), design and page make-up all by Veloce Publishing Ltd. on Apple Mac.
Printed in Croatia.

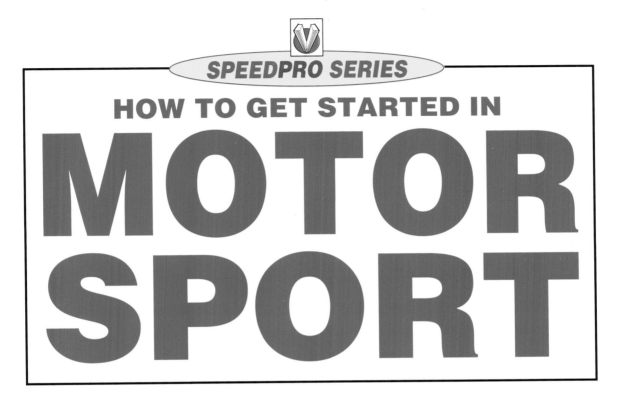

SPEEDPRO SERIES

HOW TO GET STARTED IN
MOTOR
SPORT

S.S. Collins

VELOCE PUBLISHING
THE PUBLISHER OF FINE AUTOMOTIVE BOOKS

Veloce *SpeedPro* books -

ISBN 1 903706 76 9

ISBN 1 874105 76 6

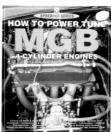
ISBN 1 903706 77 7

ISBN 1 903706 78 5

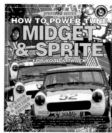
ISBN 1 903706 78 8

ISBN 1 903706 75 0

ISBN 1 901295 62 1

ISBN 1 874105 70 7

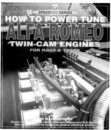
ISBN 1 903706 60 2

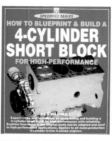
ISBN 1 874105 85 5

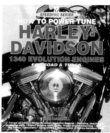
ISBN 1 874105 88 X

ISBN 1 901295 26 5

ISBN 1 901295 07 9

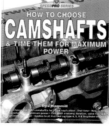
ISBN 1 901295 19 2

ISBN 1 903706 73 4

ISBN 1 874105 60 X

ISBN 1 901295 76 1

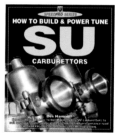
ISBN 1 903706 74 2

ISBN 1 901295 80 X

ISBN 1 901295 63 X

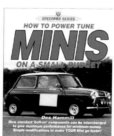
ISBN 1 903706 07 6

ISBN 1 903706 09 2

ISBN 1 903706 17 3

ISBN 1 903706 61 0

ISBN 1 903706 80 7

ISBN 1 903706 68 8

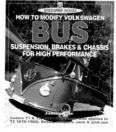
ISBN 1-903706-14-9

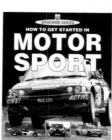
ISBN 1 903706 70 X

- more on the way!

Contents

Foreword, author's note &
  thanks 7

Introduction 9
What is club motorsport? 9
A potted history of club motorsport ...9
Who runs it 10
How to join 10
The Motor Sports Association 10

Chapter 1. Competition licences ..11
Explanation of MSA competition
  licences 11
Personal experience 11

Chapter 2. Safety equipment 14
Fire extinguishers 14
  Hand-held 14
  Plumbed-in 15
Cut-off switch 15
Roll cages 16
Seats 16
Harnesses 16
Racewear 16

Chapter 3. Flag signals &
  symbolic stickers 18
Flag signals 19
  Blue 19
  White 19
  Yellow 20
  Yellow/Red striped 20
  Red 20
  Orange/Black quarter 20
  Green 21
  Black/White diagonal 21
  Black with Orange disc 21
  Black 21
  National 21
  Green with Yellow chevron 21
  Chequered 21
Stickers 22
  The novice cross 22
  Extinguisher 'e' 22
  Cut off 'lightning bolt' 22
  Tow markers 22
  Driver's name 22
  Club stickers 22
  Numbers 22
  Tape 22

Chapter 4. Autocross 23
History 24
Cars - normal classes 25
  Class A - Economy Production
    Saloons 25
  Class B - Rally cars up to 1650cc .25
  Class C – Rally cars over 1650cc .26
  Class D – Cars up to 1650cc 26
  Class E – Cars up 1650cc 26
  Class F – Cars over 1650cc 26
  Class G – Specials 26
  Minicross 26
Basic equipment 26
Personal experience 27
Autocross advice 29

Chapter 5. Autotesting 30
History 31
Car - normal classes 32
Sample paperwork 35
Test diagrams 35
Basic equipment 35
Personal experience 35
Autotesting advice 37

Chapter 6. Karting **38**
History 38
Normal classes 41
   Single engine, four-stroke Pro
   Kart 41
   Twin engine, four-stroke Pro Kart 42
   Two stroke 100cc TKM 42
Basic equipment 42
Personal experiences 42
Karting advice 43

Chapter 7. Motorsport officials **44**
Marshals 45
Scrutineers 45
Clerk of the Course 46
Stewards 46
Marshalling advice 46
Recommended equipment 46
Personal experience 47

Chapter 8. Motor racing **51**
History 53
A rough guide to racing clubs 57
Common classes 57
   Open wheeled 58
   Closed wheeled 59
   One make series 59
Racing line: explanation and
   diagrams 59
Basic equipment 60
Personal experience 60
Race car construction diary 62
Motor racing advice 69
First event 69

Chapter 9. Rallying **70**
History 71
Stage rallying 76
History 76
Basic equipment 77
Sump guard 77
Personal experience 78
Rallying advice 80

Chapter 10. Road rallying **81**
A note on 12-car rallies 82
The car 83
   Noise 84
   Lighting 84
   Bodywork 84
Basic guide to navigation 84
   Map references 87
   Tulip diagrams 87
   Herring-bones 87
   Grid lines 87
   Spot heights 87
   Symbols 87
   Departs 87
Basic equipment 88
Rallying personal experience 88
Road rally glossary of terms 88
Road rallying advice 90
Scatters 91
Scatters personal experience 91

Chapter 11. Speed events **95**
History 96
Car - normal classes 103
   Road saloons & sports cars 103

Road-going kit & replica cars 103
Modified production cars 103
Sports libre cars 103
Single-seaters 103
Basic equipment 103
Personal experience 103

**Chapter 12. Student
motorsport** **106**
History 107
Personal experience 110

Chapter 13. Trials **112**
History 113
Car - normal classes 115
   Production car trials 115
   Sporting trials 115
   Classic trials 116
Basic equipment 116
Personal experience 116
Trials advice 119

Chapter 14. What car? **120**
Cars the author's gone clubbing
   with 121
   1985 Volkswagen Golf CL 121
   1985 (rebuilt 2000) Ford Fiesta
      XR2 121
   1986 Volkswagen Golf GL 121
Track days 121

Glossary of terms **123**

Index **127**

Foreword, author's note & thanks

FOREWORD

For years I had known about the old circuit up on the hill and wished that it were still in use. One weekend my wish came true and my life was changed forever ...

Watching cars drift through north tower bend was something I thought I would never see outside of vintage films. I was very wrong, but then being wrong was a hobby of mine as, at that time, I seriously wanted to be a Grand Prix driver.

I didn't find club motorsport - it found me. The event was the first Crystal Palace sprint run by Sevenoaks and District Motor Club, the first time I saw real racing cars up close; a revelation to a 16 year old boy. It had a profound effect on me as, alongside the classic Lotuses and Metro 6R4s, were a bunch of standard road cars of the type I was intending to buy in a few months' time, after my seventeenth birthday. I vowed to myself that, as soon as I could, I too would drive at Crystal palace!

About a year later I went to college and my forgotten vow was remembered as one of the lecturers, Richard Smith, was a keen club racer, and I went along with him to a few events to play at being one of his mechanics. All was going well and, as soon as I passed my driving test, I bought myself an old banger of a car, joined the motor club and entered it in a small rally. Suffice to say we (a long-suffering friend of mine agreed to navigate) finished last, but the bug had bitten me. I started entering as many events as I could and the college agreed to lend me a car to race at Lydden. I needed my race licence and, for a college project, wrote about the process of gaining it. That was, I suppose, the start of this book and the beginning of a new chapter in my life.

Before I go into detail I want to cover some basics that you may or may not already know.

Firstly, I'd like to dispel the myth that motorsport is expensive; it doesn't have to be. To be a competitor you don't need to be Ayrton Senna or own a Ferrari - all you need is a car with an MoT and road tax. What you do and how much you spend is up to you. Some people spend tens of thousands of pounds a year to try and win a small metal cup; others spend less than a hundred pounds and stand a chance of winning some of the same small metal cups and various championships. The thing I love about amateur motorsport is that anyone can win; super, experienced star drivers who spend a king's ransom can be beaten by novices in totally standard road cars bought for under a thousand pounds.

Motorsport is seen as a sport for the rich but, in reality, it is a sport for the people. It doesn't matter if you have all the driving talent of a citrus fruit, the important thing is that motorsport is the most fun you can have with your clothes on! If you don't want to risk your car but you like to spectate, then why not take up marshalling? You get right up close to the cars and drivers, and the best bit is it costs you nothing at all!

If you ever fancied having a go at motorsport but thought you couldn't for one reason or another, wake up, read this book and GO CLUBBING!

AUTHOR'S NOTE

I expect that, when this book is published, there will be some who wonder why a certain detail of their particular sport has not been included. The book is intended as a beginners' guide and, as such, contains only the essential information needed to start participating and gain experience.

Some disciplines have not been covered: drag racing, grass track and rallycross amongst them; short oval racing, also known as stock car racing, also. This is because a standard car can't take part in these sports and survive. If it were possible, I would love to do a full bore second edition covering these.

THANKS

Putting a book like this together involves the help of a number of people, and I would like to acknowledge and thank the following: Richard Smith, Paul Boast, Harry Leggett, Chin, Colin Shipway, Mark Dawson, Andy Manston, Oliver North, Bill Boddy, Bob Di Nozzi, Mark Hughes, Dr. John Upham, Colin Billings, Nicky Thomas, Martin Howell, John Vigar, Pat Toulmin. Also the following companies, organisations, etc: Sevenoaks and District Motor Club, British Racing and Sports Car Club, Formula Brookes Motor Club, Motorsport, East Surrey College, Playscape Pro Racing, Club 100, British University Karting Championship, MSA, ACSEMC, ACSMC. www.Vintagekarting.com supplied the early karting pictures. Andy Manston of M&H Photography supplied the superb photos in the rallying section. For more of Andy's great pictures visit www.m+hphotography.co.uk.

Colin Shipway of Sevenoaks and District Motor Club supplied many of the Autotesting and Speed pictures.

S.S. Collins
North Kent, England

Introduction

WHAT IS CLUB MOTORSPORT?

Club motorsport is the name given to amateur motorsport, so-called after the many motor clubs and drivers' clubs that organise the programmes, which range from tiny local events with very few competitors to massive affairs with literally hundreds of cars and thousands of spectators. Venues can be large, purpose-built circuits like Brands Hatch and Silverstone, or a muddy farmer's field somewhere outside Dorking. Some of the best drivers in the world compete regularly at the three types of venue mentioned (yes, even that muddy field), and the great thing is, you can, too!

A POTTED HISTORY OF CLUB MOTORSPORT

A long time ago in France a bunch of chaps thought it would a jolly good wheeze to drive their new fangled automobiles as fast as they could against each other - and now we have club motorsport in Britain, too! Well, actually, there's a bit more to it than that.

At the dawn of time (as far as a car nut is concerned) in France in the 1880s, many informal reliability trials were run for the motorised contraption that German engineers Karl Benz and Gottlieb Daimler came up with, the winner was the guy who broke down last. This carried on until 1894 when a French magazine organised a run from Paris to Rouen. More than 20 cars took part and 16 finished the event. Unremarkable as that event may seem, it was the birth of a new type of sport: motorsport.

Soon, the 'Automobilists' were forming clubs in order to run events, the most famous British example being the Royal Automobile Club which met on Pall Mall in London. It's a far cry from the Bell public house in Kemsing, but something had begun.

The sport grew quickly with clubs springing up all over Europe and closer to home in Britain, too, where motorsport is - as are many things - a Victorian invention. Pioneers of club motorsport, with typical late Victorian zeal, formed the very first clubs; even students were forming them. By the time Brooklands was built the clubs were well and truly established.

The First World War halted things for a while, but, through the '20s and '30s, more and more clubs sprang up. Then, once again, German intervention stopped things from progressing. By the end of the 1960s, however, nearly every town in Britian had an active club.

The sport was started by amateurs and is still today almost entirely made up of people driving for fun. In recent years there has been a slight decline in the number of active competitors; in some areas this has caused clubs to close their doors or amalgamate with other clubs. The reason for this decline is simple: no-one knows that club motorsport exists as it has been happening out of the public eye. Which is one reason why I've written this book.

WHO RUNS MOTORSPORT?

For any type of motorsport you want to get involved in, the very first step is to join a motor club recognised by the British branch of the FIA, which is known as the MSA (Motorsports Association). These motor clubs organise and run all sorts of motorsport events, and help out on those organised by others (did you ever wonder where the British Grand Prix gets its trackside marshals from?). To compete in any form of motorsport in the UK you must be a member of one of these clubs. There are around 800 clubs in Britain and each has a different atmosphere and way of doing things; your most local club may not be the best one for you to join so do some research first by going along to club nights and events.

The FIA is the international motorsport governing body, organising world championships such as Formula One and World Rally. Every country which has motorsport has a national governing body that organises national championships. In the UK it is the MSA, which organises series such as

the British Formula 3 Championship and the British Rally Championship.

The UK is divided into 15 regions and each of these has its own association. The regional associations are formed from a number of member clubs. Regional associations organise regional championships such as, in the case of the Association of South Eastern Motor Clubs, the successful Rally 2002 championships (co-promoted with the Association of Central Southern Motor Clubs).

Motor clubs are, on the whole, locally based and promote small events for other local clubs. There are many highly competitive and successful local championships such as the Sevenoaks and DMC's Marketing Machine speed league

HOW TO JOIN

Joining a club couldn't be easier or cheaper. If you don't know where your local club is, the MSA will put you in touch. Also, many clubs are now online and a good place to start is the http://www.Ukmotorsport.com website. They have a list of all UK club websites, and a lot more besides.

Membership fees are normally in the region of £10-£20, although being a racing member of some of the big national clubs, such as the BRSCC, can be a lot more expensive.

THE MOTOR SPORTS ASSOCIATION (MSA)

The MSA is the governing body of the majority of four-wheeled motorsport in the United Kingdom. Around the dawn of motoring sport at the close of the 19th century, the development of the car led to the 1897 formation of the Automobile Club of Great Britain and Ireland. The ACGBI became the Royal Automobile Club, the main body capable of organising motorsport events. Between the time of the formation of the RAC and 1974, the RAC competition committee effectively ran motorsport. A full and complete judicial system was put in place to give competitors a right of appeal through a legally qualified body, 'the stewards of the RAC.' Between 1975 and 1979 the system was overhauled and the competition committee was replaced by the RAC motorsports council. The RACMSC became a committee of the Motor Sports Association, and was designated the MSA's sporting commission. It was formed in 1977 as the administrative and financial side of motorsport. The MSA (having dropped the RAC from its title) currently has over 700 member clubs and over 30,000 competition licence holders.

Chapter 1
Competition licences

A lot of motorsport events do not require you have anything more than club membership and a valid driving licence, but some require special licences in order to drive and navigate. These licences are issued by the MSA and can entail driving and theory tests.

EXPLANATION OF MSA COMPETITION LICENCES

The MSA issues four basic types of competition licence: the Clubman's, National B, National A and International. The cheapest licence is the Clubman's and the most expensive the International. In practice the Clubman's licence is not really worth the money as there are almost no events that require them; club membership will usually suffice.

The really important licence is the National B, which is the only licence you will really need for club motorsport as most National A and International events - such as the

British touring car championship and Formula three - are professional level.

There are four basic types of National B licence: non-race, race, stage rally and kart. The race National B covers all national B events except stage rallying and is generally the one to go for. To obtain the non-race National B you need only apply to the MSA and pay the fee (around £30). Things are a bit more complex for the other three, however. All require a medical and a driving course, which are known by the names of the groups of racing schools that run them; ARDS for racing. BARS for stage rallying. and ARKS for karting. The following section is a guide to securing one of these licences, and my experience of the ARDS course for the most versatile of all the 'B' licences, the National B race licence.

PERSONAL EXPERIENCE

Driving race cars is a demanding

pastime which takes both time and money. To race in most series in Great Britain a driver will require a number of things, the most important of which is a National B racing licence. To acquire a National B a driver must first contact the MSA to purchase a £2 booklet that contains the order form for the 'go racing' pack (costing around £40). The pack contains some adverts for racing products, a copy of the 'blue book,' an instruction video, a couple of motor racing equipment catalogues and, of course, the race licence application form. The form has two main areas: the medical section and the practical section.

I applied for and received my 'go racing' pack and promptly marched down to my GP to book a medical. The medical was going well (do I have all my limbs, do my internal organs all work in roughly the correct fashion, etc.) until it came to the eye test, and a slight worry troubled me; I'm a bit colour blind. This prevented the doctor from appending his much-needed autograph to my form. He did, however, do an in-depth colour vision test and sent the results to the (and I quote) Chief Medical Examiner of the Royal Automobile Club of Great Britain Motorsports Association, or, in other words, another doctor. About a week later I got the thumbs up and so it was off to Castle Combe to prove I could drive a race car.

I had to sign on at 8.30am. Ouch. I arrived in a dripping wet Wiltshire to be told that the circuit was at its most treacherous as it had started to dry and become really slippery. I handed my application form in to the secretary and sat down to my theory test.

There was nothing very taxing about it. First, it tests you on the flag signals used by marshals to communicate with drivers; yellow for danger, blue overtaking flags, and so on. Then there's the common sense section, what to do if your throttle sticks open, how you should behave if you are understeering off, etc. I passed with a perfect score - well, I am writing a book on the subject!

Then came the bit that worried me. It clearly worried all the others there, too. Ten or so laps in a Ford Focus. Ten or so laps which would get me a race licence or would get me a 'good try, better luck next time.' This worried the two businessmen, it worried the kart champion, it worried the two grass track racers - and it really worried me!

After a few laps with the instructor driving it was my turn. I put my feet on the pedals of the modern car for the first time and - miraculously - they felt identical to those in my 16 year old Golf, even the steering was heavy, just as I liked it. Things were looking up. Castle Combe is a typical British airfield circuit in the same vein as Silverstone, Snetterton and Pembrey.

Crossing the start/finish line in fourth gear, heading at a rate of knots towards the first turn, a fast right-hander called Folly, I would have taken this flat-out but for the wet conditions; a slight lift would keep me on the safe side. This was, after all,

just an assessed practice. Burying the pedal quickly up towards Avon Rise, the circuit got very bumpy as I concentrated on keeping the car stable. Almost instantly Quarry Corner was upon me. I turned in late with resultant understeer as I left my

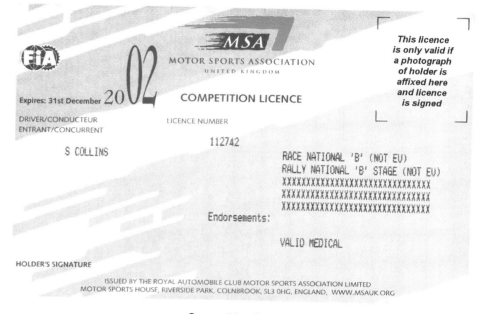

Competition licence

DATE	CLUB	CIRCUIT	FORMULA	EVENT	GRADE	O/ALL-CLASS RESULT	AUTHORISED OFFICIAL
6.5.02	RMC	LYDDEN		SPRINT	NATB	5/5.	N. Slwed.

UPGRADING SIGNATURES

2002

DATE	EVENT	OFFENCE/PENALTY	AUTHORISED OFFICIAL

PENALTY RECORD

DATE	VENUE	INJURIES	DOCTOR	DATE CLEARED	DOCTOR

MEDICAL RECORD

IMPORTANT In the event of an accident, the M.O. must enter the Medical Observation of any significant injuries suffered, and if deemed serious return this licence to the MSA. For conditions of issue, validity and upgrading requirements see Competition Licence Notes 2002.

braking a little late. Dropping down to 3rd gear on the bumps unsettled the car a bit as well, "try something else next time," I thought to myself. Down farm straight into 4th gear before braking for the esses. Back into 3rd I heeled and toed then turned in, clipping the rumble strip on the apex of the bend, winding off the lock in preparation for Hammerdown, a flat-out, right-hand kink. I didn't know quite where to shift to 4th here; the perfect place would be on the apex but that would be a bad idea as it would really unsettle the car and, at this speed, would not be a good idea. I shifted before I got there.

Out of Hammerdown now, I charged towards Tower Corner, braking with the car travelling in a straight line. Using my big toe on the middle pedal and blipping the throttle with my little toe, I selected gear no. 3; I loved this corner already as it involved jumping the kerb. I looked towards the Bobbies chicane and stayed in third (just) before braking. As Castle Combe is really quite devoid of any reference points on this section a cone marks the correct turn-in point, a luxury I knew I wouldn't have when I raced here. The chicane is fun as I put two wheels up on the rumble strip kerb.

On the exit I got hard on the power and ran wide out onto the other kerb. Flat-out through Westway Curve and it was time to start thinking about Camp Corner, putting a wheel up the kerb on the inside and then again running out wide following the ideal racing line. Along past the pit wall and into a new lap. Time to consider taking Folly flat-out this time ...

I passed the driving test and, within four weeks, was the proud owner of my very first National B race licence.

Chapter 2
Safety equipment

The ex-Mini. It cannot be too strongly stressed just how dangerous motorsport can be, as this mid-'moment' Mini demonstrates. (Courtesy Andy Manston)

Motorsport can be a dangerous pasttime and, even with all the modern safety measures, drivers are occasionally injured or worse. To reduce the number of injuries the MSA and FIA set certain safety standards with which cars and drivers must comply. These safety measures are very rarely needed but vital, nonetheless. This equipment tends to be fairly costly, but the more you spend the safer you will be

FIRE EXTINGUISHERS

Although fire is rare in modern motorsport it's still a risk, so all cars must carry extinguishers. There are two types of extinguisher systems, plumbed-in and hand-held. The pros and cons of both are as follows.

Hand-held
The main advantage of these is that the driver can discharge them directly at the source of the fire. They are also far

cheaper to buy than the big, plumbed-in systems, and lighter and far easier to install, as they are held in a quick-release bracket. However, a major disadvantage is that they are located within the car so that if the driver is knocked out or becomes disorientated, the marshals cannot operate the extinguisher. They also tend to have a smaller capacity than the plumbed-in systems, and cannot be discharged into the engine bay from within the cockpit: those few seconds getting out and round to the engine bay may mean a few hundred pounds (or worse) in damage.

Plumbed-in

When the trigger on these is pulled the contents discharge onto the driver's upper body area and into the engine bay; some systems have additional nozzles that also direct the contents to the area of the fuel tanks. When installing a plumbed-in system, care should be taken that the trigger cables are not kinked, or form an S-bend. The tubes through which the extinguisher fluid flows should not be kinked for obvious reasons. On a mechanically triggered system 'total discharge' valves should be fitted.

The best method of triggering a plumbed-in system is electronically. The triggering circuit should have its own power source and a way to check whether the system is operational. At the race circuit plumbed-in extinguishers should be armed with the pin removed at all times when on track and in scrutineering, and also at all times during rallies when helmets are required. An inoperative extinguisher will be reported to the clerk of the course for penalisation of the team/driver for contravening safety regulations. Extinguishers are checked during scrutineering and often whilst the cars are in the holding area.

Cut-off switch and fire extinguisher pull.

The plumbed-in type of extinguisher is expensive and heavy, and installation is fairly complex. However, it is far superior to hand-held bottles and, in that respect, far safer.

CUT-OFF SWITCH

All cars that race and stage rally in the UK must be fitted with a cut-off switch on the exterior. MSA regulation Q8 states: 'The circuit breaker, when operated, must isolate all electrical circuits with the exception of those that operate fire extinguishers. The triggering system for the circuit breaker on saloons should be situated at the lower part of the windscreen mounting, preferably on the driver's side or below the rear window. On open cars it should be situated on the lower main hoop of the rollover bar on the driver's side or as above. Alternatively, on historic vehicles the mounting point may be situated vertically below the line of the scuttle on the driver's side.'

Q8 also explains that the switch must be marked with a red lightning bolt on a blue background and white border, and must also have the on and off positions clearly marked.

On some cars the cut-off switch is placed in a cut-out on the wing, although this is very rare. The advantage of this is that if the car ends up on its roof with the driver unable to reach the switch, the marshals can quickly access the switch and reduce the fire risk. However, if the car is involved in a spot of close racing that gets a bit too close, the wing could deform and make the switch inaccessible or inoperable. If the switch is placed on the windscreen base area and the car is on its roof, it would take a brave marshal indeed to climb under a car that may be about to catch fire (the extinguisher trigger is always next to the cut-off).

At a race meeting a car will go through safety scrutineering before it get out on track. During this procedure it is normal to check the cut-off switch.

The scrutineer asks the mechanic to start the engine and then he turns the switch to the off position; all being well the systems shut down and the engine stops.

ROLL CAGES

Stage rally and racing cars must have rollover protection in the form of an approved roll cage. A roll cage is simply a structure of steel bars inside the car which prevents the driver from being crushed should the car overturn. An additional advantage is that it can prevent a car being written off by a heavy impact.

Fitting a full roll cage is perhaps one of the most challenging tasks in motorsport as it should be made to fit a car exactly. The Blue Book has very strict standards on roll cages and how they should be fitted into the car; this is because your cage is probably the most likely thing - apart from your crash helmet - to save you from serious injury in an accident.

Roll cages are manufactured by a number of companies around Europe, and one or more of them will make a cage for your model of car. It's a fairly

expensive item (generally over £200), which takes a fair while to be delivered, but it is an integral part of the competition car. If you intend to compete on a regular basis in any discipline, it's worth considering one.

SEATS

Special competition seats are a necessity for race and stage rally cars, as they, too, improve safety. These bucket seats are comfortable and should prevent 'submarining.' Competition seats range in price from around £100 to thousands of pounds. If you are just starting off in motorsport there's probably no reason to buy a super expensive pair of seats; instead buy a pair of cheap clubman's seats. Another option is buy some secondhand seats which could save you a lot of money. Competition seats also have slots for racing harnesses to pass through.

HARNESSES

The racing harness is a glorified and much more effective seat belt than the standard item, which is designed to

keep you firmly in your seat under all circumstances. The seat belts in your average road car are of the three-point type; this means they are attached to the chassis at three points. Competition belts, generally, are attached at four or six points. Both four- and six-point harnesses have straps which go over each shoulder and two around the waist, all four meeting in the middle where a fighter jet-style, quick release buckle connects them. Six-point harnesses also have two crotch straps that come up between your legs and meet at the buckle. These crotch straps have been the cause of much discomfort to male competitors over the years when – well, I expect you can guess ... There are MSA guidelines on fitting these belts.

RACEWEAR

In many events the car's crew must wear fireproof overalls and crash helmets to protect themselves from fire and head injuries. Gloves and boots are also recommended. It's worth being fitted for these at a shop as comfort is essential. A half-decent set of racewear should last a few years (barring mishaps). Overalls must be worn and have the right labels that show them to be of the correct standard for competition, as specified in the Blue Book. When buying overalls for driving, visit a reputable racewear stockist (of which there are quite a few in the UK) and let the experts advise you about what to wear. Overalls are manufactured in two materials - Proban or Nomex - the latter being the better and more expensive.

Crash helmets are, perhaps, one of the most recognisable items in motorsport. They're available in various price ranges, with some

A harness sits on a competition seat awaiting an occupant

The moment you start to think about safety equipment. (Courtesy Colin Shipway)

costing over £2000 and some as little as £60. There are two basic types: open-face and full-face. Open-face helmets cover the entire head except for the face. They are used mostly these days in rallying and by the occasional saloon racer; open-faced helmets are generally a bit cheaper than an equivalent standard full-face. Full-face helmets are what most drivers choose. They cover the head and face completely with just an aperture for the driver to see through; strong polycarbonate visors cover these apertures so that the head is completely protected. Full-face helmets are safer than open-faced.

Helmets are strictly regulated by the MSA, and must carry the relevant stickers placed by the manufacturer to show that it has passed the tests carried out by various watchdogs. The required standards are within the Blue Book. The helmet must then be checked by a scrutineer who will, if he considers the helmet to be of a suitable standard, affix an MSA approved for motorsport sticker on it.

Fireproof gloves and boots are strongly recommended, too, for safety reasons and the fact that, though driving shoes or boots may look like 1970s trainers, they are specially designed for race driving and will probably improve your driving.

Racewear is expensive but motorsport can be dangerous so it's money very well spent.

Chapter 3
Flag signals & symbolic stickers

Red flag: racing stops.

FLAG SIGNALS

Flag signals are an important part of motorsport. Marshals wave coloured flags at competitors to communicate signals to them. The most famous of all of these is the chequered flag and, if you follow the flags to the letter, you are likely (if your car holds together) to see it at the end of the race.

As you may have seen watching motor racing on TV, organisers signal drivers from the side of the track by way of colour-coded flags. There follows an explanation of the colours and what they mean, and how to respond to them. Flags have two states: stationary and waved. A waved flag can have a different meaning to a stationary flag. When a flag is waved at you, you must respond.

Blue

Stationary: another competitor is following close behind
Have a look in your mirrors so you know where the following competitor is and work out where they're likely to try and pass. If you can signal with your hand where you want them to pass, do so.
Waved: another competitor is overtaking you.

A faster car is overtaking you. You should give the other car space to pass. Sometimes a blue flag is waved when it should be stationary but, as a rule of thumb, if you are shown a blue flag - waved or stationary - a faster car that is probably a lap or more ahead of you is trying to pass. Let it through (this may involve moving off the racing line and losing time).

White

There is a slow moving vehicle on the track. The flag is waved at the start of the sector that the slow vehicle is in.

This is a fairly rare flag to see; it's often used in the immediate aftermath

The novice cross is clearly seen on the back of this stock hatch Peugeot.

of a nasty shunt when an ambulance is on the track, or when a car with mechanical difficulty is trying to get back to the pits. If you see this flag, be aware that there could be an incident, or you could be forced off the racing line. Caution is essential.

Yellow

Stationary: danger ahead; slow down to a speed where you can be sure that you have full control of the vehicle. No overtaking.
Waved: great danger; slow down considerably, expect to change from the racing line or even stop. Again, no overtaking.
Yellow flags are often a contentious subject, from grand prix racing down to the smallest kart race. It's usual for drivers to acknowledge a 'yellow' with a raised arm, but to continue at unabated speed. This practice - whilst understandable - is dangerous and irresponsible. There are often marshals on the track and by not slowing drivers endanger them as well as themselves.

Yellow/Red striped

Stationary: slippery surface ahead.
Waved: slippery surface imminent
This flag is commonly known as the oil flag, and is shown whenever there is something on the circuit affecting grip. When this flag is shown drivers should back off.

Red

Racing is stopped. Slow down and continue in the direction of racing back to the pits or starting grid, following marshals' directions. There is no overtaking permitted. Be prepared to stop as the track may be blocked. In speed events, abandon your run. The red flag is shown mainly when there has been a serious accident and a car is stuck in a dangerous position. Sometimes it is shown when medical assistance is required. In racing it tends to be bad news, although in speed events it's fairly commonly used as there are no yellow flags.

Orange/Black quarter

This flag is used by organisers to avoid using the red flag in the event of a major incident that could be cleared up without stopping the race. The flag is shown first to the leader as he crosses the start and finish line, who slows to around 80kph. The field forms up line astern and follows round in the order it started in. The lead car effectively becomes a pace car until the green flag is shown at the start/finish line and racing recommences. During the time the flag is being shown there's no overtaking and drivers must keep to

Cut-off switches

Headlights taped up.

the pace set by the leader.

Green

All clear, shown at the end of a danger area (yellow), after the orange and black quartered, and at the start of the warm-up lap. Green flags are also waved from all marshals' posts on the first lap of each session and also on the warm-up lap. On the first lap of a circuit drivers should note the positions of all marshals' posts.

Black/White diagonal

Shown along with a car's number, this flag is bad news, as it means that the driver's behaviour on track is not up to scratch and he is being closely observed by officials; he may be black-flagged if the behaviour continues. You should never, ever have this flag shown to you if you drive well and responsibly, but then the red mist could get anyone. If you are shown this flag, take it easy, it's being done for a reason.

Black with Orange disc

Shown along with a car's number, this flag indicates a mechanical problem or - worst of all - a fire that the driver is not aware of. The driver must call at his pit on the next lap. However well you prepare your car you can never be certain that something won't go wrong on track, especially with newly-prepared cars. If you're shown this flag, go into the pits and get one of your pit crew to look over the car. If a problem can't be found, ask a marshal.

Black

Shown along with a car's number, this flag indicates the end of a driver's race. The driver should return to the pits, park and report to the clerk of the course.

This flag is used for serious breaches of driving standards, rules, and other infringements. Again, you really should never have this flag waved at you, but it does happen.

National

Used often in rallies, the National flag is used to signify the start of an event although it's used less and less; I've only been started by the Union flag once.

Green with Yellow chevron

Jumped start: only used in kart racing

Chequered

Shown at the finish. Cease driving at high speed.

STICKERS

Almost all competition cars carry stickers of some sort on their bodywork, with the notable exception of most road rally entries. You will need to know what they look like and what they mean. Most are needed for racing and stage rallying only, but it's worth knowing them all.

Club stickers.

The novice cross
Used by competitors who have accumulated less than 12 signatures on their competition licence. Displayed on the back of the car.

Extinguisher 'e'
This sticker is placed next to the extinguisher pull on plumbed-in systems

Cut off 'lightning bolt'
Placed next to the cut-off switches both inside and out.

Tow markers
Towing eyes must be marked in a colour distinctive to that of the surrounding area; the towing eye must be indicated by an arrow also. Next to the arrow should be the word TOW.

Driver's name
This must be the name of the person driving, also if you decide to display blood type make sure its correct as it could save your life!!

Club stickers
Most race and rally series require you to carry a sticker of the club's logo, and a championship sticker which often carries a sponsor's logo.

Numbers
These are the most obvious stickers required. competition numbers must meet the standard defined by the MSA in the Blue Book: black numbers on a white background are mandatory.

TAPE

In all types of event it's worth taping over the battery positive terminal and taping the negative terminal in yellow tape. In most high speed events it's worth taping over the headlights so that the glass or plastic does not shatter all over the track and cause a hazard to others should you come into contact with something solid.

Chapter 4
Autocross

Mud flies on a local Autocross event as Colin Anderson, driver of the 'Honiton Special', applies an armful of opposite lock.

This chapter is not about that odd, North American version of Autotesting that we know in Britain as Solo 2, but in the states is known as Autocross.

No, this chapter is about mud, horsepower, opposite lock, head-to-head racing and yet more mud.

I'll be honest here and confess that I wasn't going to include Autocrossing, partly because I didn't really know anything about the sport, and what I did know reminded me of a lesser form of stock car racing. I thought this right up until a couple of members of my club decided to have a go at a local event. They had a great time and showed me the pictures. I later read a report on the event in the club magazine; it seemed it was something I had to have a go at.

This odd discipline is a mix of grass autotesting, rallying, motor racing and sprinting. Cars are raced around a course marked out in a field as fast as possible. It's similar to grass 'testing' but the tracks are wider, longer and more flowing which allows the motor racing elements of Autocrossing. The competing cars start side-by-side up to four at a time, 'racing' each other around the course. The sprinting element comes in here as the order the cars cross the line bears no relevance to the overall

Sand-o-cross at Weston-Super-Mare is spectacular, as this Mini demonstrates! (Courtesy Andy Manston)

results, which are calculated on the time taken to complete the course, the fastest time being the winner.

A fast start is crucial in order to get in front of a quicker competitor, making it hard for him to pass and therefore achieving a better time. So why is there a rally element? Partly because large proportions of Autocross cars are actually rally cars of one sort or another, and partly because the driving style adopted is superb practice for loose surface stage rallying. This sport, as well as being a rally training ground, is the starting point for many participants in Rallycross, Autocross's big brother.

HISTORY

Autocross came about during the postwar resurgence of motorsport in the early 1950s. Motor clubs had started holding events that involved timed runs around courses laid out in farmer's fields. In the South West of England the sport was noticeably growing in popularity; Taunton motor club reacted to this and became the leading club in British Autocross when it was the first to organise a series of Autocross events in 1954. The South West claimed another first again via Taunton MC when, in 1959, the club was awarded a permit to organise and run a national event.

Autocross had served its apprenticeship as a discipline and, by the '60s, regional championships had started to occur. The sport enjoyed peak popularity right into the '70s. The regional association championship events attracted spectators of up to three thousand, and usually around 80 competing cars. A totally unique

This rather tired Alfa Romeo was bought for less than £500 and driven to and from events. The car was scrapped after the engine faile

Autocross-style event had evolved on the beach at Weston-Super-Mare, where four cars run abreast in the annual (it still runs today) Sand-o-cross organised by Weston's motor club.

In recent times Autocross has been in something of a decline, possibly due to the rise of the rival Autograss, and possibly due to a lack of knowledge about the discipline. At the time of writing, entries are low and spectators almost unheard of, apart from the odd passer-by walking his dog. However, there are still strongly supported regional championships and one of the most notable is the joint

ASWMC and ACSMC series.

CARS - NORMAL CLASSES

Autocross classes are defined in the Blue Book, which means that most events run the same class structure, a fact, perhaps, that sprinting could take note of. Cars range from the mundane to the totally and completely bonkers, barking mad. The same could be said of the driver's, in fact ... The class regulations are all fairly open compared to most other motorsport disciplines. However, every club and region has its own little nuances, so this is just a rough guide.

Class A - Economy Production Saloons

Once again, the normal shopping car class. These are generally fairly standard cars, but with quite a few avenues for modification. However, totally standard cars do fairly well most of the time. Something worth thinking about buying in this class is a set of 'knobbly' tyres for your driven wheels, though not essential.

Class B - Rally cars up to 1650cc

The cars in this class are a mix of road rally cars and stage rally cars. It's often frequented by the omnipresent Minis

Two Ford Escort 1600s duelling right to the finish.

This big 2.9-litre Sierra oversteered in a spectacular fashion.

(who actually have their own version of the sport in Minicross). Peugeot 205s are also common

Class C – Rally cars over 1650cc
The same as above. Many of the bigger-engined Peugeot 205s compete here as well as bigger machinery.

Class D – Cars up to 1650cc
Cars in this class have their engines mounted above the driven wheel.

Class E – Cars up 1650cc
Front-engined rear wheel drive.

Class F – Cars over 1650cc
The big 2-litre rear wheel drive Ford Escorts are common in this class.

Class G – Specials
These cars are fairly mad-looking, homemade, single-seat, purpose-built racers. This class also includes four wheel drive vehicles, which may incur a 5 per cent penalty.

Minicross
A rather serious class for specially-prepared Minis. It offers very, very close competition (often a bit too close!) and exciting racing. Minicross is actually a clubcross class that tends to run alongside Autocross events.

BASIC EQUIPMENT

A car with the following:
   mudflaps on all four wheels
   hand-held fire extinguisher
   adequate seat and belt
A national B non-race licence or better.
Flame retardant overalls (of MSA standard).
Crash helmet (of MSA standard).
Valid club membership card.

This 2.2-litre Subaru Legacy incurs a 5 per cent penalty for being four wheel drive.

PERSONAL EXPERIENCE

My first Autocross event started in my front room. I searched the Internet to find the next local Autocross event within reasonable distance of my home. Central Sussex MC was running its annual event just under an hour's drive away, so I printed off the entry form, completed it and sent it to the organiser.

The next stop was that useful, but somewhat inconsistent tome, the Blue Book. According to section G (specific regulations for Autocross and Rallycross), the only modifications I needed to make to my road car were as follows: fitting mudflaps behind all four wheels, taping across the headlights so they don't shatter on impact, and mounting a medium-

The somewhat insane 3-litre 'Honiton special'.

Minicross cars are immaculately prepared.

Double-driven Alfa Arna.

sized, hand-held fire extinguisher. I left fitting the mudflaps until the last minute but found that my drill was not working the night before the event and I couldn't bolt on the flaps. Minor panic resulted in my fitting the front pair of flaps via a combination of gaffer tape and Superglue very early the morning of the event. I headed off to the venue, a field just outside of Haywards Heath.

The rear mudflaps I fitted in a pub car park near the venue using the same method employed for the front pair. Within five minutes of leaving the car park, the newly-attached rear pair parted company with the car, so I turned around to go back for them. I finally got to the start venue half-an-hour after scrutineering should have started. Luckily for me, only five other competitors were there and the organisers hadn't finished setting up. I parked between a rather interesting special and a Mark I Escort.

I got chatting to the owners of the Escort who turned out to be a bunch of nice chaps from Haverfordwest in Wales, though were, rather oddly, members of Bournemouth MC. They'd driven down the night before the event, a journey that had taken them eight hours.

After my meeting with the Welsh brigade and scrutineering (the scrutineer didn't notice my lack of rear flaps, phew!), I went to check out the opposition: a rather tasty-looking Lancia Delta turbo and a rusty, double-driven Alfa Romeo Arna.

I was advised to walk the 1200 metre course, so I did. The layout was basically an oval with a couple of S-shaped complexes in the middle of the two straight sections. The track was marked around the inside with little white flags and around the outside with blue ones. The circuit was very bumpy in a couple of places,

A minicrosser.

especially on the approach to one corner where a lump on the racing line would force front wheel drive cars to understeer away from the apex.

I was looking forward to the four-car start, but it wasn't to be. The cars were to be on track in batches of four, starting in pairs twenty or so seconds apart. I was to be in the first pair of starters, after the Minicross event that was running at the same time, had finished its practice session. The other half of my pair was the rusting Alfa and following us onto the track would be the turbocharged Lancia and one of the Welsh chaps in the Escort.

The flag dropped and we were off. I got a slightly better getaway on the damp grass than the Alfa, but down the straight he took the lead as I struggled for grip. The first lap seemed to be a case of stringing a series of 'moments' together as I fought to keep the car travelling (if not pointing) in the right direction. My time was clearly not going to be a fast one as I had no traction whatsoever. Towards the end of my run I saw the Welsh Escort in my mirrors and decided it was prudent to allow him through, considering the way he was driving. This I did and finished my run. The more experienced competitors complemented me on my getaway. I watched the second runs of both the Welsh Escort and the rusty Alfa with the rest of the Welsh contingent. I came to the conclusion that they were absolutely barking mad.

The Alfa returned to the paddock with a very sick-sounding engine and retired from the event, I was promoted to second in class by default. The event was very laidback and I was enjoying a late summer afternoon in the best way I can imagine - pounding around a track at high speed. On my third run I lost control going over the large bumps mentioned earlier, the car snapped out of control flat-out and I fought to bring it back, all arms and elbows for a second before I recovered it. I went on to set my fastest run yet that time. Crossing the finish line and returning to the paddock, I was greeted by a marshal holding my left front mudflap. I swore mildly at the things that had caused me no end of problems all day.

On my final run my car was damaged, though only cosmetically - one of the bigger bumps had ripped off my front spoiler. It took only a minute to put it back on, though, so I wasn't worried.

I drove home feeling that I'd had a good day on an event that was really non-damaging to the car. I will be back for sure.

Autocross advice

"Try starting in second gear for better traction off the line."

"Keep it on the island."

"If competition is close you could try and hold up your nearest rivals."

"Just go for it and don't expect to drive home."

"Fit your mudflaps before the event!"

"If you are taking it seriously then it's worth using a trailer to bring the car to the event, as this is an off-road sport and breakdowns are common."

"If you plan to do a few events invest in a set of knobbly tyres for your driven wheels."

Chapter 5
Autotesting

205 Rallye passing through a 'gate.' (Courtesy Colin Shipway)

The Mini is well known for its autotesting prowess. (Courtesy Colin Shipway)

What kart racing is to formula one, Autotesting is to professional rally driving, and is where many of Britain's top drivers - including 1995 world rally champion Colin McRae - started out.

Top autotesters can claim they are the most spectacular drivers in motorsport as they flick, turn and slide their cars with acute accuracy through the tight course of traffic cones or poles. Like many disciplines, 'testing is all about racing the clock. Cars run singly around ultra-tight courses, relying on handbrake turns and reverse flicks to negotiate the difficult courses. Events are run on both tarmac and grass, with the latter being cheaper and more usual.

Autotesting is, perhaps, the cheapest form of motorsport with entry fees starting at around five pounds and no modifications to the car; wear is minimal so all you need is a car. Age is no barrier, either, with drivers as young as 14 years old able to start in production autotesting (with a passenger). Fairly often they beat older, more experienced competitors! The quickest cars on autotests are very rarely the most powerful; more often, the better handling, shorter wheel base cars such as the Mini dominate.

HISTORY

On an Oxford motor club gymkhana in 1925 the following test was included as part of the day's events: "A series of four posts will be arranged at an equal distance apart, hoop–la rings and coconuts will be placed on the posts. The entrant who dislodges the coconuts and impales the rings on his 'sword' in the fastest time will be the winner." Was this the birth of

Classics can be competitive - but this one wasn't! (Courtesy Colin Shipway)

Autotesting? Probably not, but it's a nice foreword to the history of the discipline.

In 1934 the organisers of the Ulster rally decided to include a timed driving test on their event. The driving test started a trend on rallies that continued after the war. The tests occurred more and more on rallies and were usually manoeuvrability sections marked out with cones or stakes. The sections often involved a garaging or parking style test where cars would have to be stopped in a given space. The tests were timed against the clock. This small tie-breaker section of a rally was becoming a highly popular discipline in its own right.

In the sixties there was a series of televised driving tests which attracted respectable audiences and some of Britain's top drivers of the time, including Paddy Hopkirk. In 1970 these driving tests became known as Autotesting to avoid confusion with the learner driver test that frightens 17 year olds more than any other exam!

Autotesting has become a common, low cost event run by many motor clubs, and even a British championship.

CAR - NORMAL CLASSES

Cars are normally standard production types with little or no modification. The most common trick is to lower tyre pressures to give better grip on grass. It's well worth clearing out all the junk that accumulates in the back of the car as you don't really want it flying around the boot as you compete. Top competitors in the MSA British championship often use 'sawn-off'

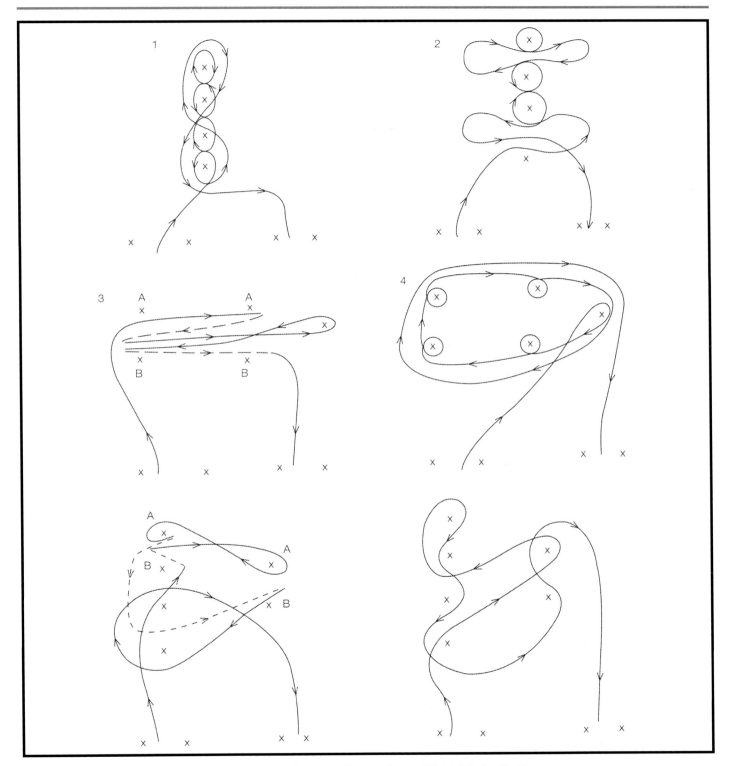

Test diagrams. (Courtesy Sevenoaks and District Motor Club)

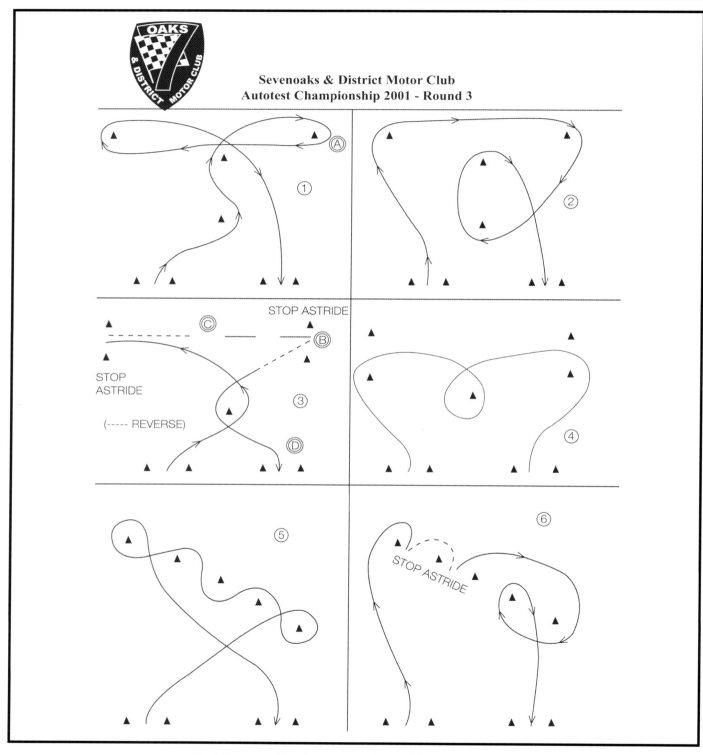

Test diagrams. (Courtesy Sevenoaks and District Motor Club)

Minis. Classes vary from club to club, but are often based on the dimensions of the cars rather than performance.

SAMPLE TEST DIAGRAMS

On the accompanying diagrams (taken from a Sevenoaks and District Motor Club event), the triangles represent cones or poles. The line is the course to be driven, the dotted and shaded sections should be undertaken in reverse gear. Stop astride means that you must bring the car to a complete standstill between the cones before continuing. None of the test routes are longer than 200 metres.

Point a
The fastest way to negotiate this turn is by using the car's handbrake to slide

the back out and 'flick' the car around

Point b
The car must stop exactly at this point.

Point c
As the next section is taken in reverse the driver must turn the car through 180 degrees as quickly as possible.

Point d
The finish box; the car must stop inside this box, the clock stops when the car does.

BASIC EQUIPMENT

A standard road car.
Club membership card.
A good handbrake.
National B competition licence (if a

national B status event).

PERSONAL EXPERIENCE

My first Autotest, I don't mind admitting, was a bit of a disaster although I had a great time. Sevenoaks Motor Club runs an evening series of Autotests for members of the Weald Motor Club (a consortium of Sevenoaks and other local clubs). The event was of the non-damaging grass type and was being held in a pair of adjacent fields in the North Downs - not far from Brands Hatch.

There was a reasonable entry as the fee was only £5, and I didn't have to pay that as, at the time, I was under 21 years of age! Already I was enjoying competing on an event where not only was entry free, I didn't

Weekday events often run at a local level and take place in the evening. (Courtesy Colin Shipway)

Cars range from everyday classics to modern models such as this Ford Puma. (Courtesy Colin Shipway)

spend any money on fuel either as the venue was close to my home.

At signing on I was given a card with my car number on and spaces for the marshal to fill in the times I took to complete individual tests. I was also given a piece of paper with the 6 test diagrams. The tests didn't look too frightening, and only a couple required reverse gear. Each course or test could be attempted twice.

The first course I attempted was quite simple - on paper. I rolled up to the starting box and passed my time card to the marshal, who, it turned out, was the reigning champion, and was told to go in my own time. I selected first and tried to make a fast getaway but instead just crept forward

with my front wheels spinning like crazy. I rapidly came to the conclusion that driving on grass is quite different and requires a delicate right foot ...

I attempted the course twice and managed to knock off five seconds from my time the second time round. The next run was where it turned into disaster. On coming up to the first gate, two cones close together, I managed to take out both of them while understeering far too much. Through the next few runs I discovered a few things: my 'new' handbrake wasn't as good as I thought; Golfs understeer amazingly (actually, I knew that already, but we won't go into that!); the understeer seems to come and go as it likes, and

something always goes wrong.

The first of the more difficult runs I tried involved going from first to reverse and back again. I loved it, the car didn't. Braking into the finish area I was hotly chased by a cloud of exhaust fumes, brake dust and a horrible smell of burning clutch. Pulling away to drive back to the paddock area I heard/felt a slight knock from under the bonnet but ignored it and and did a couple more runs. I attempted what looked to be a difficult run and tackled the course with some attitude. Sliding the car out of the last turn I was applying armfuls of opposite lock until I realised that the front of the car was pointing directly at the finish box. I nailed the throttle and

The startline. (Courtesy Colin Shipway)

then slammed on the brakes to bring me to a stop in the box. The marshal was writing my time on the card, "Quicker?" I asked, "A lot quicker," came the response "a good run." It turned out I was fourth quickest on that test.

With two more runs out of my twelve to go, I went to the line, where started to feel and hear a huge knocking and banging from under the bonnet. I took it back to the paddock and had a look - one dead engine mount: game over. Still, I managed to drive the thing home. Oh, and I finished last ...

The next season I entered the entire series and was again dogged by small mechanical problems. The tests are not that hard on the cars but do show up any mechanical weaknesses. But they're great fun and there's nothing much to hit apart from a few old traffic cones.

Autotesting advice

"Always get a run in on all the courses as soon as you can as conditions could change and you could lose a lot of time."

"Take everything you don't need out of the car so there is nothing loose in it."

"Take a tarpaulin along with you so when you take your stuff out it doesn't get wet from the ground or the sky."

"On grass, lower your tyre pressures substantially as this will give you more grip."

"Take a foot pump along with you otherwise you can't pump up the tyres again after you let the air out of them."

"The power of the engine does not always decide the winner; smaller cars such as the Mini always do better than a Golf or an Escort."

"Try to make sure you get the right route; a slow time is preferable to a wrong route."

"If you can walk the tests before you drive through them it always helps when trying to remember the route."

Chapter 6
Karting

Anyone with an interest in motoring knows what karting is; in a nutshell, motor racing with much smaller cars. It's also where almost all of today's top international racing drivers started.

Karting offers drivers a chance to show their skill in fairly equal equipment. Karting always provides close wheel-to-wheel racing and often a lot of action. Because much of British kart racing is overrun by professionals and those trying to be professionals, coverage of the discipline is limited to the thriving 'arrive and drive' scene. Although bad attitudes and unsporting behaviour is common, the 'arrive and drive' series can be the most fantastic fun.

There are two types of kart track, indoor and outdoor. There are indoor circuits everywhere and they are very cheap to drive at; outdoor circuits are generally more expensive but worth it as the karts are often quicker and you get to race in different weather conditions. The outdoor tracks are

longer, too; some up to 1600 metres.

There are also two types of kart, the heavier and slower four strokes and the rather rapid two strokes. It's probably worth doing a few sessions in a twin engined four stroke before trying out a faster two stroke.

HISTORY

Karting is a purely American invention.

In 1956 an experienced hot-rodder and racing car builder called Art Ingels built a simple little vehicle that was strong enough to carry his weight. The small engine provided the drive to just one wheel via a bicycle chain. All those present at its first test in a local car park were surprised when Ingels shot across the car park at what is universally known as 'a fair old lick.'

The next year a group gathered in

The first ever meeting of karters assembled in the car park of the Rose Bowl Stadium. (Courtesy www.Vintagekarting.com)

a car park in Pasadena with a number of similar machines; this meeting is thought to be the first of a group that later became known as karters. The vehicle closest to the camera in the picture on the previous page is an example of what was known as a GP Muffler and not one of Art Ingels' creations; two of which are to the left of the GP Muffler.

Some of those at the meet saw karting as a new direction for motor racing, and twelve of them agreed to form an organisation fashioned after the sports car club of America; the organisation became known as the Go Kart Club of America. The new club secured a venue at which to hold races, a shopping centre car park.

In 1958 the first dedicated Kart manufacturer was founded by a pair of exhaust company partners. The company was called the Go-Kart Manufacturing Company Incorporated. (A commercial artist hired by the company to advertise its product coined the name Go-Kart.) The kart engines were acquired from a defunct lawn mower company and the first karts were in kit form. The sport exploded and Go-Kart Mfg was getting around 30 orders a day for its product.

By the early sixties, however, after a large but unsuccessful takeover bid, Go-Kart Mfg went bust, even though the industry was booming with over thirty kart manufacturers.

Karting had started to spread its wings and racing facilities were being established around the world. In 1958 the Trokart - believed to be the first kart available to the public in the UK - went on sale in Britain. Soon karts were being manufactured in the UK.

Stirling Moss being a director of the Keele Kart company.

In 1959 Master Sergeant Mickey Flynn organised the first significant British kart meeting at the USAF base at Lakenheath, and another event took place at Onchan the same year. The airbase meeting was a huge success with works Team Lotus grand prix driver Graham Hill participating.

The year after the events at Lakenheath and Onchan a Buckler kart was allowed a few timed runs at the Great Auclum Hillclimb, a round of the British championship. The brilliantly named David Bosher-Jones, in an 1100cc Cooper, set BTD, taking 20.49 seconds to complete the course. All eyes were on Peter Hilton (manager of Buckler Karts), however, in one of his company's 197cc karts, who managed to complete the same

The first ever kart was a amazingly simple contraption and the obvious ancestor of today's karts. (Courtesy www.Vintagekarting.com)

Rental karting is the cheapest and arguably the most fun form of karting.

Single engine, four-stroke Pro Kart.

course in 24.43 seconds. The kart's competitive time caused embarrassment to many in the racing car arena, and some attribute the RAC ban on karts in speed events to this performance.

There's an interesting postscript to the Auclum story involving the kart-based Trackstar of the late 1980s, which ran on British hillclimbs before the RAC really tightened the regulations to ban karts from speed events, that can be read about in Chris Mason's excellent book 'Uphill Racers'. British karting exploded with the advent of 'arrive and drive.' Martin Howell ran the first commercial 'arrive and drive' event in the UK in 1985 at

a circuit in Tilbury. Howell supplied the karts and all the equipment needed to run the event, and the drivers simply arrived and drove. He was onto a winner and 'arrive and drive' became a permanent fixture at many UK circuits; indeed, some circuits were created simply for 'arrive and drive' karting.

These days almost every large town in England has its own karting venue. Old bus garages have been redeveloped into indoor kart centres, and small circuits are springing up everywhere - even in a big tent in London's Docklands. There are even touring 'arrive and drive' championships, and the best of these

is run by Club 100, using TKM two stroke karts. The Club 100 series tours the national level circuits such as those at Buckmore Park and Rye House, providing low cost and highly competitive motorsport.

NORMAL CLASSES

The three main types of kart most likely to be encountered at 'arrive and drive' events –

Single engine, four-stroke Pro Kart

Heavy but easy to drive, the single engined kart is common on indoor circuits, and shorter, outdoor venues often use them. They have top speeds of around 40mph. A single-engined Kart is pictured on the previous page in one of its natural habitats, the indoor circuit.

Twin engine, four-stroke Pro Kart

Similar to the single-engined kart, the twin is far more common on longer outdoor circuits. Most of the national karting venues will have a fleet of these for corporate 'arrive and drive' events. They have top speeds ranging between between 60 and 80mph, depending on quality.

Two-stroke 100cc TKM

The ultimate in 'arrive and drive.' 100cc, two-stroke TKM karts are chain-driven, direct drive, and must be push-started. They are far harder to drive than Pro Karts and far quicker; in a spin or stop the engine will most likely also stop. They have top speeds approaching 90mph and will out-accelerate some cars.

BASIC EQUIPMENT

One of the fantastic things about 'arrive and drive' karting is you just turn up at the circuit and it's all laid on for you. Everything you need to take part will be available, and is usually included in the cost of kart hire, though I recommend you buy your own helmet and overalls. Special competition licences are not needed for 'arrive and drive' either. Karting is really very cheap. I found that a proper pair of racing boots really do improve your driving and allow taller drivers to sit lower in the kart.

PERSONAL EXPERIENCES

The first time I competed in a decent quality 'arrive and drive' karting event was at Buckmore Park in Kent. The event was running what is known as a grand prix format, a number of short heats with random grids; the results would be collected and the quickest drivers would go through to a final.

I arrived at the circuit and signed on with a couple of guys from work. We were directed to suit up in overalls and helmets and then to a drivers' briefing. In the briefing the clerk of the course went through the basics of the racing line such as safety and how to drive a kart.

Before the heats we had to go out for a few practice laps to settle into the karts and learn the newly extended (so I was told) circuit. I was allocated a number, as were the other drivers, about thirty in all. I had an early number and was directed via a tannoy system to a kart in the middle of a pack of about ten twin engine, four stoke racers. I jumped aboard, the engine was started and, without hesitation I was off.

The first corner was a fast double apex right-hander that led onto a short straight. The lap continued with a fair selection of different corners, including a terrific, fast, sweeping downhill section. I was slightly shocked and a little scared by the speed at which the thing accelerated: I suppose that was how Art Ingels must have felt the first time he drove his prototype in the fifties. Under braking, the kart seemed to know that the circuit was taking a right turn and, under heavy braking, the thing pulled hard right. I soon worked out that only the right wheel was doing any braking when I braked on the straight to see what would happen and spun. I returned to the pits and jumped into a spare kart just in time for the first heat.

The race got under way and I was in the middle of the pack at the end of the first lap when one of the engines developed a misfire; by the end of the next lap I was last and losing touch. I remained in that poor position until the end of the heat. After that first heat I was advised by another competitor to try and take the first corner flat out. I decided to have a go at this as the extra speed would provide an opportunity to overtake on the run into the hairpin.

After I had removed myself from the tyre wall on the first corner of the first lap of the second heat, I set about chasing the pack. I caught some of the slower runners and ended up finishing a few positions from last.

I hoped for a somewhat better performance in the third heat. I started the race from second on the grid and managed to drop only three positions by mid-race. Going through the first corner I started to close the gap on the kart in front. By the same corner on the next lap I was crawling all over the back of him. I had a look into the second apex but, after my earlier shunt, decided against making a move. I got a good run out of the hairpins, we were side-by-side through the downhill sweeps and then I was ahead! I took the ideal line into the fastest section of the track, a near flat fast kink. I moved across the track and then disaster struck: I hadn't entirely passed the other kart and we touched. My kart speared left at top speed and shot over the rough broken concrete on the outside of the circuit. It lifted off the ground slightly and dropped back to the ground at the rear end. The shock transmitted up my spine and I felt the bones compress. The kart continued out of control with me as a passenger and stuffed itself into a tyre wall. I hesitated before clambering to my feet and saw a marshal running to my aid; I waved to show that I was okay. The next day my back was very stiff and I had some big bruises: a

Club 100 kart.

direct result of my rather silly couple of shunts.

There was still another heat to go and I wanted to try for a decent finish. I was even keener when I realised I was to start from pole position. The flag dropped and I lifted my left foot off the brake whilst opening the throttle with my right. I got the start just right and led into the first corner. At the end of the lap I was still holding the lead. Apparently all hell had broken loose at the first corner and I noticed one kart in the same tyre wall I had visited earlier! I allowed myself a quick glance over my shoulder and I saw only one kart. I couldn't believe I was leading and started making little mistakes, running wide here and there. Soon the one kart that was behind me was angling to get past. The threat seemed to focus my driving and I stopped making errors. I held onto the race lead, with the other kart constantly trying to pass - or so I thought. It turned out I was racing my own shadow ... The final lap was amazingly tense as I was desperate to win. I saw the chequered flag drop - I had won! Unfortunately, I didn't do well enough to qualify for the final but was happy to have won a heat.

I go karting on a regular basis, still, and my driving has definitely improved since that first crash fest at Kent's finest karting venue.

Karting advice

"When you start you'll be rubbish, but persist and your speed will improve with experience."

"No-one is quick out of the box; well, not unless your name's Senna."

"Stay calm, even if you get hit by someone else."

"Drive with your head."

"Walk the course if you can,"

"Oversteer slides are fun but are not fast."

"It's very easy to overdrive the kart; stay cool, relax and don't try too hard, you'll never remember your best laps."

Chapter 7
Motorsport officials

Marshalling; silly hats are optional

Rally marshalling. (Courtesy Colin Shipway)

This chapter deals with all of the officials that ensure motorsport events run smoothly. As a competitor you will at some point cross an official of the meeting; remember they are doing what they are for a good reason.

MARSHALS

Marshalling is a rewarding activity, not financially, but through the sheer satisfaction of doing a hard day's work and helping an event to happen. Without marshalling there would be no motorsport.

The role of the track or stageside marshal is to ensure the smooth running of his sector of the venue. This can involve ensuring that spectators are not standing anywhere dangerous, keeping the track surface clean or - perhaps as a flag marshal - signalling to the drivers. Often on a marshal's post a designated observer is in charge of the post and reports to the clerk of the course.

Marshals may be allocated (by the chief marshal) a notorious 'action' spot, such as the 'yump' at Longcross or Paddock Hill curve at Brands Hatch, where accidents are frequent. They may also be allocated a bleak junction or control where very little happens.

Whether in orange overalls behind some ARMCO, in yellow tabards in a forest, or perhaps even wearing waterproof jackets at some isolated control, marshals are there to run the event. Every motor club in Britain is happy to take on new marshals; just contact your local club.

I marshal at a few events each year as I compete on a regular basis - and you do get the best view!

SCRUTINEERS

Scrutineers check that competing cars are free of safety, eligibility and environmental problems, and is an job for the more technically-minded. Scrutineers are often the bearers of

Marshals are exposed to all weathers and should dress accordingly. (Courtesy Colin Shipway)

bad news when a car is found not to be up to scratch, or has a problem. All scrutineers are trained in their own kind of apprentice scheme.

CLERK OF THE COURSE

The clerk of the course is in charge of the entire meeting, responsible for the organisation and running of the event, and decisions of a safety or judicial nature. It's not unusual for the Clerk of the Course to have deputies and assistants to help him do what is a

fairly complex and stressful job.

STEWARDS

As a rule of thumb most events have three stewards, two club stewards and one MSA appointed steward. The MSA steward must ascertain that the venue is safe before the event can start. In some situations competitors can appeal to the stewards about decisions made by the Clerk of the Course. At the end of a meeting the stewards send a report to the MSA that

could (if the report is negative) determine whether or not the organiser ran future events.

MARSHALLING ADVICE

Recommended equipment
British motorsport events take place year round, and marshals are exposed to all weathers. Waterproofs, warm clothing, woollen hats, sun lotion and sun hats are all essentials and will be regularly used, often on the same day! On my personal marshalling checklist I

Marshals get close to the action.

have the following items. (By the way, I don't actually have a checklist and I tend to forget the whole lot!)

Waterproof jacket, waterproof trousers, woolly hat, jumper and gloves to contend with the British weather.

Avoid wearing manmade fibres as they can cause nasty burns if they start to melt in a fire or if left leaning on a hot area of car. It sounds silly but it happens.

A whistle; these are commonly used in rallying to signal the approach of a car. A Day-Glow tabard is often a marshal's uniform of choice but these are usually supplied by the organiser. A good pair of work boots are worth

investing in as, not only do they provide protection from the elements, but also from liquids such as fuel, and possible crushing as you will probably end up in close proximity to heavy cars. I know what you're thinking, competition cars are anything but heavy. Get one on your foot, though, and I think you'll see my point ... Ear plugs are advisable to avoid returning home with a head that feels the size of a balloon.

A pair of good, strong scissors or a hunting knife is recommended as part of the MSA's new spectator control programme. Just joking; they're nothing to do with crowd control but are useful to have,

especially in an extreme case where it may be necessary to cut the seatbelt of a trapped driver.

With all this other preparation don't forget about food and drink for yourself. Often, clubs supply an events marshal with a bag of goodies, but it's probably best to take a packed lunch and a couple of litres of water to avoid dehydration.

PERSONAL EXPERIENCE

The ninth month of 2001 brought the super 1600 works rally cars to Kent. Sevenoaks and DMC had teamed up with two other local clubs to bring the Formula Rally series to the Barretts

Fire marshals at the ready. These marshals are in black as they are from Silverstone

Rally of Kent. I pitched up to a rather run-down looking barracks on a raised section of land between the Thames and the Medway.

The timing of the event was a little unfortunate; barely a week after the terrorist attacks in the USA, and it was fairly obvious that the military had more to worry about than some rally cars running around the base. Arriving at the main gate I had to provide proof of my identity (fortunately, I had my driving licence) and sign my name in a logbook, watched by a rather stern and very intimidating officer. Then a younger soldier escorted me back out to my car and proceeded to search it whilst two others stood by with SA80 assault rifles at the ready. I enquired about the state of these weapons, and was informed rather cheerily that they were loaded.

I was beginning to wonder whether marshalling was such a good idea after all, when a member of the club introduced himself to me as someone I had spoken to on the phone on an earlier occasion. He gave me two packed lunches, a Day-Glo tabard and a chequered flag. He then pointed to a group stood by a Land-Rover and instructed: "Go over there and tell them you are on the finish line." I wandered over and was given a brief rundown of the dos and don'ts of rally marshalling. Then it was off to

Startline marshalling at Crystal Palace.

the flying finish line with a bloke called Roger and a chequered flag.

My job on the finish line - which was on the exit of a fast, righthand bend preceded by a long straight - was to alert Roger, who had the flag, when a car was approaching. The finishing times recorded by the cars were to be clocked, when Roger dropped the flag, by the timing crew who were sitting at a control about two hundred meters down the road.

The plan was simple, when a car was approaching I would shout this information to my new chum and he would raise the flag. The raised flag was the signal for the timekeepers to be ready to clock the finish times. The system had one fatal flaw which revealed itself when David (or is it Mark - I always get them mixed up) Higgins came through driving the course car, a fully kitted-out group N Subaru Impreza gravel rally car. My

shouts that a car was approaching were lost in the popping and yelping tones of the turbocharged car's exhaust note. We decided, therefore, that when I saw a car approaching I would shout and raise my arm, if two cars arrived together I would raise both arms and Roger would signal the time control in the same way. I wish I had remembered to take that whistle I had acquired at the Notting Hill Carnival a few weeks earlier (the only event for me that takes precedence over motorsport!).

Standing on the outside of the fast turn I felt a little vulnerable so made myself a bit of an escape route through the undergrowth. Roger (a very experienced marshal, who, as it happened, was standing a few feet back from the tarmac's edge) was taking the mickey out of me for this as he thought the cars would be nowhere near me. In the event, he was right ... The first car to appear at the far end of the straight was the works Ford of Francios Duval, I signalled to Roger that he was coming and, as planned, up went the flag. Next thing I know there's a rally car flat out (very quick indeed) with all four wheels on the inside of the corner. Being an older chap, I was surprised that Roger could move as fast as he did. Instead of dropping the flag, his upper body froze whilst his lower body moved quickly backwards with the result that Roger found himself on his bottom with a broken flag.

I'm sure that Duval lost a second on his time as the flag didn't drop, it didn't matter, though, as he dominated the event. If you ever want a good laugh watch the TV coverage of the event (which is on the Formula Rally video) and you will see from Duval's onboard camera Roger running backwards with the flag held above his head.

The rest of the impressive super 1600 field came and went without incident, although there were a couple of long delays which told us a car had gone off elsewhere in the stage. The one make cars contesting the lesser Ashford Rally came next, bringing with it some very secondhand looking Peugeots and Volkswagens amongst other, pristine examples of the same machines. These cars were a little bit dull and, to be honest, I was getting bored when, suddenly, my attention was grabbed by a screaming, ex-world rally championship Mitsubishi Lancer being hotly chased by a Subaru. The amateur competitors had arrived in the form of the Kent Forestry Stages rally, this clubman's event has an amazing selection of machinery ranging from seriously quick, ex-world rally cars to modified production cars, far more interesting than even the formula rally cars.

The day was good fun and on the second stage we marshalled the course, which was run in the opposite direction to the first. I was waving a new chequered flag (after Roger's mishap). The cars returned but were far less in number as many had fallen off in the forest stages or succumbed to those ever-present gremlins. At the end of the day I returned home tired but pleased to have been involved with such a good event. These days I marshal as much as I can when I'm not competing and still enjoy it.

Chapter 8
Motor racing

A Formula Ford pack at Castle Combe in Wiltshire, England.

Brooklands, the birthplace of British motor racing, now a sad monument to the past. Recently, a major car manufacturer submitted plans to develop the area.

Two Ford Zetec cars await their next session.

Motor racing is, perhaps, the most famous and evocative of all the automotive sports, and I could trot out all those old, tired clich s about man and machine in passionate battle - but won't. But racing cars is one of the best things you can do without removing any clothes!

The British motor racing scene is one of the strongest in the world. with thousands drivers competing every year in cars as diverse as modern formula one chassis to ageing and near standard hatchbacks. The drivers range from professional racers who devote their lives to driving cars and promoting their sponsors, to the enthusiastic but casual weekend racer that ranges from the cash-strapped student to the multi-millionaire.

That old saying - you don't have to be rich to be a racing driver, but it sure helps - is certainly true; it does help but it's far from essential although racing is expensive, compared to most other disciplines. Entry fees are constantly climbing and what you get for your money is not fantastic. However, some clubs are reversing this trend.

HISTORY

Motor racing became a distinct, separate discipline in the 1890s when French organisers of motorsport events placed the emphasis on speed and driving skill. In 1895 the first major road race took place, Competitors rode their automobiles from Paris to Bordeaux and back again.

For a while Paris became the hub of international motor racing as it was where many intercity point-to-point races started. However, these highly popular races were about to come to a tragic end.

The newspapers described the 1903 Paris to Madrid race, rather dramatically, as 'the race of death' though with some justification. Cars were reaching speeds of up to and beyond 90mph, safety standards were

FF1600, weekend racers with the family as crew.

non-existent and tragedy resulted as five competitors and a number of the 500,000 spectators were killed in a series of accidents. From this point, nearly all road racing was banned. Events were confined to closed road or, something new, special, purpose-built motor circuits.

Not long after this the racing world changed forever again, and this time it was Britain that changed it. In 1906, motoring enthusiast, Hugh Locke-King, watched the Targa Florio race and the French grand prix, both of which took place on the continent with no British entries. The reason for

this is that, at the time, the UK was stifled by a blanket 20mph speed limit, which meant that there was no way a British manufacturer could compete without having access to a permanent test and race venue. Locke-King called to Weybridge in Surrey all those of a like mind, and thrashed out a plan. Nine months later it was completed: at 3.25miles (5.23km) long, the world's first, purpose-built motor circuit - Brooklands - was finished. On July 6th 1907, *Autocar* magazine covered the birth of British motor racing in an eight-page special.

But Brooklands suffered from a

fair few teething troubles in the first few years of existence, including low race entries and - more worryingly - low spectator turnout. The doom merchants who, at the time of the circuit's opening, had forecast disaster, seemed to have been right. At the beginning of the 1908 season a meeting for amateur drivers was held at the track. Lap times were taken in the morning and the race run in the afternoon on a handicap system. Eleven competitors started and seven finished within the same one and three quarter minutes, the race was won by just ten yards. This was an exciting race

This very tidy car is a good example of a stock hatch racer

and the Brooklands executive noted this.

A private competitor list was drawn up, along with a set of regulations that included the following:

A private competitor shall have no direct interest in the automobile or accessory industry.

A private competitor shall neither enter for, nor drive in any race at Brooklands a vehicle which is the property of a person or persons having a direct interest in the automobile or accessory industry.

A private competitor shall not accept any fee or remuneration of any

kind, whether direct or indirect from any firm or individual for driving or entering a motor car in any race or competition.

A private competitor shall be entitled to enter for and drive in races, even though, by their conditions, they be open to others beside private competitors, but in races for private competitors they alone shall be eligible to compete.

This set of regulations, along with the 1908 amateurs' meeting, is most certainly the root of British clubman's racing, and also, perhaps, made motor racing a sport rather than the science

that the top level always has been.

After World War One, motorsport grew in popularity, with new circuits being constructed within the Brooklands complex. At Donington Park and Crystal Palace races were also being run. Racing was fast becoming a very popular pastime for amateurs with a few works getting involved, too.

The Second World War put an end to racing in the UK for almost ten years, and petrol shortages kept racing to a minimum for a few years after that. Brooklands had been closed at the outbreak of war, never to reopen,

The stealth B6 is an attractive example of a GT racer

and is now a sad reminder of what once was. Donington had been badly damaged by the military and was abandoned.

The war may have destroyed Britain's premier circuit but left one thing that would alter and benefit motor racing in this country forever, airfields. The USAF and RAF bases that had sprung up all over rural England and Wales were suddenly surplus to requirements when hostilities ended. Airfields at Goodwood, Silverstone, Thruxton, Ibsley, Castle Combe, Charterhall, Snetterton, and Pembrey in Wales (to

name most) were converted into race circuits over the next few years. Britain suddenly had lots of motorsport venues and a strong club-racing scene grew up around them. Everyone had the motor racing bug, so much so that even a trotting track was converted to allow racing automobiles at Mallory Park. Attitudes changed in 1955, however, when spectators were killed in a tragic shunt at the Le Mans 24 hours race in France. Safety has been a major consideration in motor racing since then.

In 1965 a new short, one mile circuit was built near Dover in Kent.

Bill Chesson's Lydden Hill circuit was the birthplace for a new type of motor racing, rallycross: as the name suggests a cross between racing and rallying with half loose surface/half tarmac circuits. The cars are rally car variants; more recently a clubman's stock hatch class has been successful.

As the years have passed many circuits have appeared and others have disappeared, such as Crystal Palace. Donington Park made a triumphant return and, under the guiding hand of Tom Wheatcroft, attracted the Formula One world championship for a second race in

Formula Ford is where professionals and amateurs meet. There's a lot of money floating around in FF, as these three cars in their paddock area show.

Britain in 1993. 2001 bought the next major racing milestone in the UK with the construction of a brand new circuit. Rockingham is a 1.5 mile, banked oval course the like of which has not been seen in Europe since the closure of Brooklands.

A ROUGH GUIDE TO RACING CLUBS

Only a few clubs in the country organise motor racing events due to the costs involved. These clubs are generally much larger and far more expensive to join than the local clubs. The three main amateur clubs are:

British Automobile Racing Club (BARC)

British Racing and Sports Car Club (BRSCC)

750 Motor Club (750MC)

These three clubs are not the only organisers in the country but they are the biggest. One other organiser is the South East Motor Sports Enthusiasts Club (SEMSEC), they notable for running super cheap race meetings where a competitor can get maybe three times as much track time for his money as he can with one of the big clubs.

COMMON CLASSES

Motor racing in the UK has a wealth of different classes and series for near standard everyday shopping cars to full specification, modern Formula One Grand Prix machines. Which class you choose depends on how much money you are willing to spend.

There are two types of racing car: open wheel like F1, and closed wheel

The start of the race is a busy time and there are cars everywhere

as in the BTCC. As a rule of thumb the closed wheel classes are cheaper to compete in as the cars tend to use many standard (cheap) road car parts, Open wheeled classes require special, purpose-built (expensive) racing parts.

The following is a quick guide to what's out there as there are far too many different series with their own classes to list them all here. A comprehensive (long) list is available from the MSA.

Open wheeled

Formula Ford 1600 - the starting point for many grand prix racers in the past. FF1600 is run today purely for amateurs as a more modern and professional series is run for Zetec powered cars. The 1600cc cars are run for fun by weekend racers.

Formula Ford Zetec - the expensive, professional version of the above.

Formula Honda - small, 600cc motorcycle-engined cars.

Formula Vee - these cars are based around the running gear and engine of a Volkswagen Beetle and are, as a result, cheap to maintain.

Manufacurer formulas - these series are generally seen as stepping stones for wanna-be professional racers. Often fairly high budget required.

Formula 3 - the pinnacle of British open wheeled motor racing. Recently,

Pre-race mental preparation can be as important as good car preparation

drivers who have done well in this class one season have found themselves racing in the Formula One World Championship the next ...

Closed wheeled

Road Saloons/Stock Hatch - almost certainly the cheapest classes around. The tightly regulated cars can be used as everyday runarounds (and many are). The only real modifications are to the suspension and - obviously - saftey equipment. Most of the big racing clubs run classes for cars similar to these.

Group N - very similar to the above classes but slightly more modification for racing is allowed.

Hot Hatch - fairly modified hatchbacks.

Modified Production - fully modified but still based on road cars.

Touring cars - Purpose-built, expensive and very quick.

ASCAR - a new class of racer designed to run on the fast, banked oval at Rockingham.

GT - various championships and series for high cost sports cars go under the name GT.

ONE MAKE SERIES

For many years manufacturers have known the marketing power of their product winning in motorsport; more recently they have worked out how to win every time - by ensuring that every car in the race is one of theirs. These series have dominated club racing for a few years now and every year, it seems, more and more appear. Most of the major manufacturers run 'challenge' series for their current models. When these series get dropped by the manufacturers, amateurs take on the cars and keep the championships going. These series

regulations ensure equal equipment for all competitors, although some competitors are often seem more equal than others. The tight regulations of these series do tend to keep costs down, although there's always close racing which can have costly results.

RACING LINE: EXPLANATION & DIAGRAMS

It's not really possible to learn from a book how to lap a circuit within a decent time, that comes with on-track experience and much practice. What can be learnt, however, are the basics of what is known as racecraft.

Racecraft covers everything from overtaking to the correct method of gear changing. There are many books on this subject written by those far better qualified than myself. I would recommend Ayrton Senna's *Principles of Race Driving, 1993* if you need

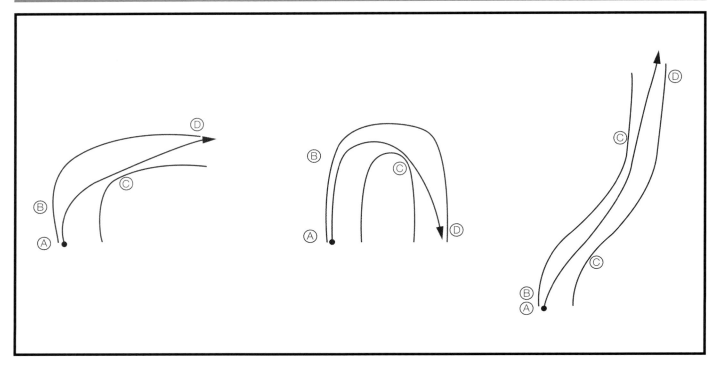

Racing line diagrams.

more information, but, to be honest, the best way to learn is to go to one of the many racing driver schools around the country and do a few laps in a road car with an instructor. What I offer here are the basics of the racing line.

Essentially, corners have three sections: the approach, the apex (or clipping point), and the exit. All three sections must be taken correctly to ensure a good speed through the corner. The three sections must be smoothly connected with the focus on exiting the corner as fast as possible. The old adage of slow in, fast out is still true in the art of cornering: enter slowly and exit at speed is the key to the game. Braking and turning points are important also but the basic line is the secret formula, if you like. If and when you do your ARDS course, this 'racing line' will be further explained, along with the two points I've just

mentioned. For now here are some basic diagrams of different types of corner and where you should position your car as a rough guide.

    A - braking
    B - turning in
    C - apex
    D - running wide on exit

BASIC EQUIPMENT

National B race licence:
Car with rollcage, competition seats, hand-held extinguisher, cut-off switch.
Helmet.
Overalls.
National B race licence:
Racing membership of a racing club; i.e. BRSCC.

PERSONAL EXPERIENCE

I sent off a large cheque with the entry form, and, a few weeks later, was off

down the M2 for the Garden of England race day weekend. I enjoy race weekends, wandering around the circuit watching the races up close is so much better than sitting in front of the TV to watch the grand prix. The paddock is an interesting place to be and generally has a friendly atmosphere. Which is all fine and dandy, barring just one thing, I was on the entry list. Cue lots of nervousness and distraction on my part, as I headed south through the Kent drizzle.

The morning mist rolled back towards the channel to reveal a scorching hot and sunny Lydden Hill race circuit, venue for my debut into the fast-paced world of race car driving. I was to drive the East Surrey College Fiesta XR2 in class E of the BRSCC Ford Saloon championship, which is a mixed bag of fairly standard shopping runabouts to heavily modified and turbocharged beasts, all of which were manufactured by the Ford Motor Company.

Once at the circuit I was really on edge; a feeling best described as that you might get from walking on thin ice - I was just waiting for something to give. Once I'd signed on I took my helmet and overalls and headed off in the race car to get everything checked by the MSA scrutineers. The ice was getting very thin now ...

I drove into the scrutineering area and removed the car's bonnet, placing it carefully in front of the car. The bonnet on most racing saloons is unlike that of a road car inasmuch as access to the engine bay is achieved by completely removing the panel, which is held on by four special locking pins. The scrutineer checked my helmet, which was new, and I was told to take it to another official to get it approved for motorsport use, which I did. This process costs just a pound and involves the safety scrutineer giving the helmet a thorough once over and putting a sticker on the side of it if it's good enough.

Whilst this was going on, the car was being given a once over to check the safety equipment was all present and correctly functioning. I trotted over to the car and climbed in, the scrutineer said all was okay and waved me out. I put the transmission into first and pulled away to desperate warning shouts: I realised the instant it was too late that I had made an almost comical error. I had run over my own bonnet, leaving it crumpled and bent out of shape. Two wide black stripes of expensive racing slick rubber now adorned the car's newly-painted orange front panel. Worst of all, almost everyone in the BRSCC had been watching and, oh, did they laugh. I was amazed at my own sheer stupidity but in a way felt that the pressure was off.

The engine was in a bad way.

Before I had fully recovered from the embarrassment of the bonnet incident, it was time to go out for practice. My first time on a circuit in a competitive situation. Sitting in the holding area, I ran over my objectives for the day's racing: to finish, stay out of trouble, let the faster cars pass (i.e. all of them), and try not to make an even greater fool of myself than I already had.

I was driving the least powerful car in the championship so would have to keep my wits about me as the more powerful cars caught and passed me. I ran about a dozen laps in the session, taking it very easy and staying well away from faster cars, which meant missing out on getting a clear lap in which to set a good lap time. My fastest lap was a fair bit slower than everyone else's in my class. I was a bit put out by being so slow but I had qualified, albeit last on the grid. After the session I found some tarmac to park the car on as the paddock at Lydden is mostly surfaced with gravel and I didn't want the stones to damage my hot, sticky tyres.

I wandered around the paddock for a while, asking more experienced drivers for tips. Then came the appointed time and I was called back to the car to get ready for the race.

At the start of the green flag lap I spun my wheels pulling off the grid to generate some heat in the tyres, and set off after the tail of a purple Escort. I was surprised by how fast the cars go on the warm-up lap and, at one point, I thought I was going to be left behind before the start! Then, pulling up to the grid, I couldn't remember where my grid spot was for a second but, before I knew it, I was in place and the red lights were on. I let the car creep forward slightly on the clutch. Green lights. Full throttle and away. I found I caught up with some of the more powerful cars on the getaway but, as soon as I changed gear, I started losing ground again. Into the first corner and

The hole where the core plug should be and ...

a screech of tyres in front caught my attention as a spinning car shot past the nose of my car.

I continued the race just trying to finish, and succeeded. After the race various drivers congratulated me on finishing, but also gave me a ticking off for being far too courteous to them and ruining my own chances! The next day one of the drivers found himself a place behind me in the race; I wasn't as courteous letting him past!

At the end of the race weekend I had finished both races, coming second in my class both times by staying out of trouble. I had no intention of breaking any records, but perhaps I didn't push myself or the car hard enough - next time I most certainly will.

One thing that occurred to me is that motor racing is a bit like a drug: every time you need a bigger and bigger hit and you become a racing junkie, sitting in the pub with your mates, discussing the best line to take through Paddock Hill bend, just waiting for your next big fix. Motorsport is seriously addictive and, once hooked, I wager you'll not be able to kick the habit for many years ...

RACE CAR CONSTRUCTION DIARY

One rather obvious essential in motorsport is a car. For most events your road car will suffice but, for racing and stage rallying, a car must be specially modified or prepared for competition. Mostly these modifications are for safety reasons but some are for performance and handling objectives.

There are two routes to acquiring a car which meets the standards of preparation demanded by the MSA: buying one that is completed or building it yourself. As with most things in life, both ways have positive and negative aspects and neither, in my opinion, is better than the other. When buying a secondhand race car, the same principles apply as buying a used car. It is certainly worth hanging around the sort of events you are interested in competing in to see what sort of cars are run, and often the paddock can be a good place to find

... the shattered valves. Note the damage on the inside of the right valve.

out about cars for sale. Talking to regular competitors is the best way to find out what you need to know to buy a used car.

Once you've bought the car you are just a quick service away from having a fully competition-ready racing car. However, buying a used car means that you are not aware of its quirks and nuances.

Building your own car is no small matter, but, by the time the car is finished, you will know every nut and bolt on it. You will know how to service and repair it yourself, it is your car and you are bound feel rather attached to it when finished, rather like a proud parent! It can be cheaper to go the DIY route but it is really time-consuming.

In order to know what goes into the build of a competition car, I joined a group of BTEC National diploma students at East Surrey college, who were about to convert an old and somewhat rotten Ford Fiesta XR2, purchased for £100, into a competitive racing car. The build took our group twenty four weeks to complete in our spare time. It could have been finished sooner but we decided to go to town on it. Every component on the car, down to the smallest nut and bolt, was replaced or restored. I kept a small diary throughout the build; here's what happened.

Week 0
The car is to be run in the BRSCC

Ford Saloon championship. To save money we intend to build the car for the class closest to a standard specification car, which is known as class E.

The series has five classes, varying from the extreme, unlimited turbo cars of class A, to the nearly totally standard Fiestas of class E. The fairly tight regulations allow us to upgrade some components to motorsport specification.

Next week we get our hands on the car for the first time.

Weeks 1-4
On seeing the car for the first time, my initial thought was "What a wreck." There was rust everywhere and it looked like it had been kept in a shed

The first time we saw the car ... What a wreck! We started stripping the interior straight away.

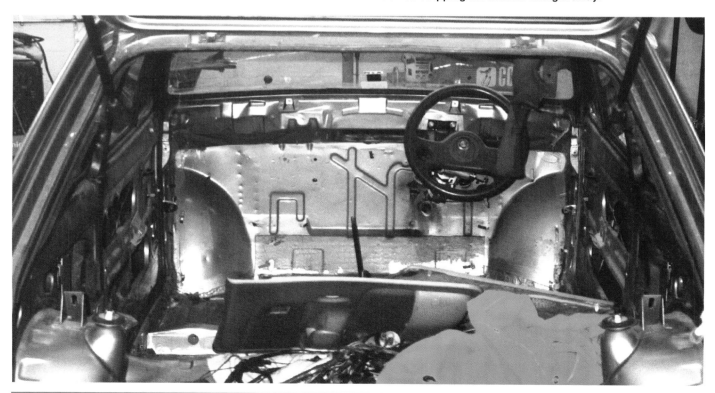

Work continued apace

The rollcage was offered up and then fitted.

Amazing progress as the engine is put in place.

Nearly there! The car is readied for its MoT.

for the past few years. We discovered later that it had ... Under the bonnet this bad situation got worse, a bit of a mess is an understatement. The cylinder head on the CVH engine had been removed and was missing, exposing the inside of the block to the elements. As a result, the pistons had rusted into the bore and the crankshaft was in dire need of a regrind. There was no way we could carry out the required engine work ourselves; we'd have to send the parts to a specialist firm to be sorted out.

The rest of the four weeks were spent stripping the car to a bare shell. Every part we removed was labelled (including every nut, bolt and washer) to make it easy to find different parts during the rebuild.

Weeks 5 -6

With the car fully stripped we got down to the rather boring task of removing the soundproofing. Manufacturers spray a hard, polymeric compound over the interior of the shell to reduce noise from the engine, loose chippings, etc. This compound has a fair weight to it so we had to spend much time scraping it out.

Under the compound we found a lot of rust holes in the floor. Some of the guys removed the rotten front wings, top mounts and battery tray, then ordered replacements.

A trolley was attached under the front of the shell to allow ease of movement.

Weeks 7–12

Before the shell was painted we had to prepare it by rubbing it all over with wet-and-dry emery paper. This was done to take the shine off of the original paintwork and smooth it both inside and out. After the rub-down we sprayed the car with primer to prevent any corrosion. The replacement parts for the front end of the shell arrived and were welded and fitted into place. Plates were made up to repair the holes in the floor. The ever-present dents in the body were filled and

The car ready to go at Brands Hatch

smoothed out. By the start of week 11, some of the rubbing down had to be repeated to remove scratches which resulted from when the car was moved around the workshop.

The hole left by the sunroof had to be filled and this was done with a strip of aluminium (which originally made up part of a filing cabinet!), riveted over the aperture.

A fortnight was almost totally spent removing another polymeric compound, this time the underseal. Underseal is used by car makers to protect the underbody from corrosion and running damage. It's a heavy and difficult-to-remove compound which took the entire team almost two weeks to scrape away. Finally, when it was all gone, we sprayed the underbody with black paint to protect it from corrosion.

Weeks 15-16
The rollcage arrived and was assembled and offered up inside the shell. Once in place, we measured up panels so it could be welded to the floor of the car. The dashboard was offered up and cut so that it fitted in the car with the cage in. The wiring loom was cleaned and restored, so the car's electrical systems are fully functional when they are put in place during the build.

Week 17
Due to the tools and other components being left in and around the car by our intrepid group and others who use the same workshop, the car developed a few unwelcomed dents and scratches. This caused a lot of problems, as the car still hasn't been painted. We spent an entire day repairing the damage, using knife putty and filler on the dents. The car was now ready for painting, hopefully next week.

Weeks 18–19
The rear axle was restored and rebuilt, with an entire new rear brake system. Literally hundreds of parts were assessed and restored or replaced if necessary. The engine block, pistons and crankshaft came back from being restored, including a rebore to the block. The engine assembly was started and an old CVH head found and restored.

Week 20

Finally, we put the car on a trailer and sent it off to the paint shop. Unfortunately, the trailer ramps fell onto one of the doors placed underneath and damaged it badly. A spare was found and rushed to join the rest of the car for painting.

Weeks 21-23

A bright orange shell now graced the workshop. The build started in earnest and, within a few days, the wiring loom and engine bay were complete. New racing suspension arrived and was assembled, then fitted to the shell, along with a new front brake set-up. The speed of progress was amazing, due to the team spending nearly an entire week on the car.

Another solid week's work saw the engine finished and installed, along with the exhaust system, brake pipes, windows and doors. The exhaust manifold needed repair as it had a crack, butt was soon fixed. Some damage was discovered on the doors - bad scratches in the new paintwork. There was much disappointment but stickers covered up the worst affected area.

Week 24

One of the students in the class had a nasty habit of bumping his cars into solid objects, and had a spare racing seat lying around which we fit inside the car. The standard road seatbelts were replaced with a four-point racing harness. All the other necessary safety equipment was put in place, too.

The car is so very nearly finished: stickers are put in place and wheels fitted so that we could adjust the tracking. With just one day left before the first race, we took the car for its MoT. It failed, so it was a rush to get it sorted out, turned around and re-tested before the end of the day. The suspension springs were not 100 per cent secure so we cable tied them in place. Also, a large rust hole was present within 300mm of a suspension mounting point. I simply can't understand why, given all the time spent under the car, no-one saw the hole.

FIRST EVENT

First time out, and it's the Brands Hatch Indy circuit, venue for round one of the BRSCC Ford saloon series. One of the students had his race licence and was to drive on this round.

In practice, the car was a little hesitant to start with but got going with a little encouragement. At the end of the session the car stalled and wouldn't start again.

Back in the paddock we found that the tyres had been rubbing on the wheelarches, leaving strings of expensive racing slick tyre wrapped around odd places such as the wing mirror and brakes. The fuel filler cap hadn't been sealing well and fuel had leaked. Both problems were rectified - or so we thought - and it was time to race.

The car was running quite well until, around halfway through, the driver was shown the black and orange flag. Fuel was still leaking from the filler cap and the car was not allowed to continue in this potentially dangerous condition.

We put the day down to experience and looked forward to the next race, again at Brands. During the race the engine blew out the core plug and dumped all its water into the cylinders and onto the track. The driver failed to notice the temperature gauge rapidly rising and the engine seized, the heat smashing the valves. Another unsuccessful day ...

Motor racing advice
"At the start of the race stay calm and try to make up some positions whilst looking out for trouble."
"Stay cool."
"When someone is alongside you, make sure you don't turn in on them."
"Make sure you are comfortable in the car and can reach all the controls easily."
"Drive with your head - you will find it's a lot cheaper than the seat of your pants."
"Have fun and stay out of trouble."
"Keep an eye on your mirrors."
"Look out for flag signals and follow them to the letter."
"Learn a circuit well before taking risks and remember you're not Ayrton Senna."

Chapter 9
Rallying

Yump! (Courtesy Andy Manston)

A sport above many others; a rough-and-tumble trial that attracts drivers to the UK from all over the world. These, in my opinion, are the real superheroes of motorsport, whose skill and daring are matched only by their stamina. Not as well equipped crews have snatched victory from bigger, richer outfits by sheer tenacity.

It's also a sport for the mechanic and office manager alike who can't wait for the weekend to come when he (or she) can have their own small adventure. This is the sport for the cash-strapped student who loves driving his tenth-hand hatchback over tight, twisting back roads and country lanes. This is the sport of great names such as McRae, Burns, Hopkirk - and a bloke called Ari. This is rallying.

There are two main distinct types of rally in the UK: the all-out, blood-sweat-and-'gears' of a stage rally, and the brain-twisting, standard car, driving road rally. The latter is cheaper and, arguably, more fun.

So what exactly is a rally? - a test of driving ability, navigation skills and teamwork. In all rallying, cars compete singly against the clock, usually setting off about a minute apart. As a rule of thumb, all rally cars must be road legal, even those that compete in the WRC, as most rallies contain road sections.

HISTORY

It's often said that the Monte Carlo Rally is the oldest rally of them all, but I have a slightly different place at which to start my rallying story.

In 1905, six years before the inaugural Monte Carlo Rally, a 'time regulated trial' took place. It was called the Herkomer Trophy and was the first international event to place importance on navigational skills and an ability to maintain a high, average

The picture says it all. (Courtesy Andy Manston)

Launchpad at Longcross, rallying can take some real guts. (Courtesy Colin Shipway)

Martin Sansom takes in some nice Forestry Commission roads. (Courtesy Andy Manston)

speed from one section of the route to the next. The event ran only twice: this year and the next. The reason for this was that the complexity of its regulations led to many protests and disputes over results. (The winner of the 2002 Rally Argentina was disqualified for having a flywheel that was a few grams too light.)

The fledgling sport died off for a bit on the international scene, only to be resurrected in 1908 by the German aristocrat, Prinz Heinrich, with his Prince Henry trial. This was a much simpler but more ambitious affair with a massive and taxing route. However, it, too, was shortlived, continuing only until 1910 when - again - early paddock politics killed it off. Although these two events were not called rallies, and would not be recognisable as such today, in reality they were the start of rallying. The emphasis was on navigational skill and maintaining

average speeds; this, combined with the special tests that both these events included, and the focus on tourers rather than small racers, was to change the face of motorsport forever.

In 1911, the organiser of the Monte Carlo Rally called Europe's motoring enthusiasts to 'rally' together in competition in Monaco during the winter of that year. 23 answered the call, the name stuck and a legend was born. The following year 87 entries started from all over Europe, from Russia to France. By 1925 the organiser had added a 80km 'trial' in the mountains above the town. This trial was perhaps the first hint of the Special Stage Rally, although the two types of rally were one, until much, much later.

For years all rallies in the UK were effectively road rallies, as we know them now, with the addition of trial and tests along the route. These small

tiebreakers became a sport of their own, Autotests.

For years British rallying carried on in this fashion until well after the second world war, although that did stop play for a while. Things, however, were about to change when a man called Jack Kemsley took over the running of the RAC Rally.

It's generally accepted that, in the UK at least, Sevenoaks and DMC member, Jack Kemsley, invented them, on the 1960 RAC Rally, the event that was the very first to involve special stages. A timed-to-the-second blast over rough, loose surface roads and tracks.

At just two miles, the Monument Hill stage introduced a whole new sport, which has since grown into - at its highest level - the globetrotting, multi-million pound circus we know as world rallying. The popular discipline that many amateurs take part in all

A Subaru in a typical stage rally scene. (Courtesy Andy Manston)

Escorts are commonplace in Rallying. (Courtesy Andy Manston)

Darren and Mark at Longcross. (Courtesy Colin Shipway)

over the UK continued to grow and develop into its two forms: stage and road rallying.

The reality was that the one 'stage' on the '60 RAC was not really 'closed' to others in the way we think of stages now. In 1961 the RAC was a forest stage rally, as we know it today. However, for years there were still road sections between stages at night, where the timing was tightened up to effectively make it a road rally section. By the mid-'60s, road rallying and stage rallying had become more separate, although special stages still cropped up on road rallies, and road rally-style sections on stage rallies until the 1970s. The special stages on road rallies at that point were said to be taken at the same speed (high) as the rest of the rally, but with the drivers wearing crash helmets.

As time went by safety considerations on special stages gave rise to new regulations that finally separated road and stage events completely. Road rallies continued as before, held on open, public roads and subject to road traffic (competition and trials) acts and regulations. Some of the more competitive sections (then called selectives) were not strictly legal. The organising motor clubs were pulling the proverbial wool over the eyes of the authorities using a special timing system.

A student at Oxford University invented this timing system and called it Targa timing. This system separates the timing from real time at each point of the event and ensures that no-one knows what time schedule the cars were running to, especially the authorities. 'Chin' of Sevenoaks and

DMC told me of a section he drove in the Calderford Rally in Yorkshire on the public highway and subject to national speed restrictions, that was Targa timed at 117mph!!

The way the regulations were written, high speed 'road races' were running with fields of up to and over 80 cars, most notably the national *Motoring News* series. The cars, on the whole, were heavily modified, very powerful and excessively noisy. Obviously, this had some effect on the residents along the rally route and soon the objectors became more vociferous. Police forces had to ban rallying in certain areas: it was clear that something had to be done - something was.

In 1988 the MSA introduced draconian regulations which covered the organisation of events and the cars that competed in them. Targa timing was banned and the 30mph average was enforced. The issuing of route information prior to the start time was out, too, so the fast 'pre-plot' events had to end. Technical regulations were tightened, banning the high-performance Escorts and Chevettes, and sign-writing on cars was outlawed.

So, road rallying had been reduced to a shadow of its former self, and the problem was: how would rallies be challenging to driver and navigator at such low speeds? The answer was navigation. Today's navigational road events place the emphasis on the navigator's skill, but still challenge the drivers as they attempt to cover the often icy and fog-bound country lanes and tracks of the UK within the correct schedule. Now drivers have to know when to drive flat-out and when to go ultra-slow.

Road rallying today is a resurgent sport with many new competitors. Welsh road rallying is acknowledged as amongst the best, even though it's a little different to everywhere else.

Stage rallying, too, is growing in popularity with the world championship that is so well televised. British amateur stage rallying has, in recent years, been stripped of its premier event, the RAC Rally. The event, now known, as the Rally GB, has become a professionals-only affair, with just cars from the world championship and junior world championship. The days of the 160-car and five-day rally over the best roads in the UK are gone, with the rally now based over a handful of stages in South Wales and no sign that this will change. Club level stage rallying in the UK is currently without a premier event. Events such as the Jim Clark Memorial Rally and the Rally of Kent aspire to this but, in fact, are a far cry from the days of the RAC. The

The Metro 6R4, a well known example of Group B was, in effect, a racing car built to run on rally stages. Williams used much Formula 1 technology and know-how in its design, so it's not surprising it was just too quick to be safe on the international rally scene. (Courtesy Andy Manston)

Classic stage rally cars can still be on the pace, such as this Escort. (Courtesy Andy Manston)

Anything goes car wise, and most cars go sideways. (Courtesy Andy Manston)

stage rally scene is still thriving, however, with a multitude of events, to the point where the motorsport press struggles to cover all the rallies that take place each week.

STAGE RALLYING

Whether racing against the clock down a rough, forest track, across a disused airfield, or around vehicle test tracks, rallying is a supreme test of driving skill. Many believe that the best drivers in the world are not the likes of Juan Pablo Montoya or Michael Schumacher, but the stars of the increasingly popular World Rally Championship.

Rally cars have two seats, however, and the co-driver often plays the most important role in a rally crew. In stage rallying, speed is the objective - to complete a stage as fast as possible - not easy when the stage

often consists of tight, twisty, gravel tracks with little margin between you and the background. The range of cars used is wide but the basic safety standards of stage cars are the highest of all amateur motorsports. The extra safety requirements are not surprising when you realise that, in rallying, there are no gravel traps or crash barriers, just trees and other solid objects that you don't want to hit.

History

Even after stage rallying parted company from road rallying, and became a high speed event of its own, it still took in some road rally-style sections linking stages at night. 1968 was a turning point for club rallying, although few appreciated it at the time. Ford had introduced the twin cam Escort, and the car soon established itself as a perfect stage rally machine. Ford's performance centre in Essex

started selling performance modification kits for Escorts and Cortinas, and so the clubman's Escort was born.

By the time of the 1969 RAC Rally, the Escort had become the stage rally car of choice for the clubman and, on the event, there were no fewer than 63 Escorts and Cortinas. The RAC Rally was still the ultimate test for the amateur, providing around 2000 miles in which to prove himself against the world's best. The Escorts were strong runners for a while until 1974 when the Lancia Stratos exploded onto the British scene, winning the RAC Rally. For a few years it was Ford versus Lancia, until in 1979 the Escort won its last RAC Rally. Ford soon stopped entering its works cars but the clubman's cars continued to become ever quicker.

In 1980 the stage rallying world changed forever with the arrival of the

Audi Quattro; four wheel drive had made its debut. The Quattro dominated until 1982 when group four gave way to group B; four wheel drive supercars had arrived. These ultra-fast and powerful cars were not meant to look pretty but ate up the rally stages of the mid-eighties with some pace. The big manufacturers were getting in on the act and the cars were getting faster and faster. A car which is now a familiar sight on club events was the Williams Grand Prix Engineering-designed MG Metro 6R4. Never has a car looked so purposeful. However, ever-increasing power and speed couldn't continue indefinitely and a series of accidents resulted in supercars being banned.

Recent years have seen a rise in the number of single venue events that keep costs down and allow for relatively easy administration. The Evo cars of Subaru and Mitsubishi are becoming new clubman stalwarts. The Escort has made a comeback, too, in the form of the Cosworth. Single venue rallying is highly popular and it's common for events to fill quickly, with reserves in the wings in case anyone should drop out.

Some rally cars are just lightly modified road saloons. (Courtesy Andy Manston)

This isn't meant to happen ... ! (Courtesy Andy Manston)

BASIC EQUIPMENT

Sump guard

Both species of rally car (road and stage) often run at some speed on rough, 'yumpy' and broken roads. This often results in the car's undersides coming into contact with rocks and other solid things. On most, but not all, road rallies this is rare, but in stage events it's a certainty.

Metal shields, known as sump guards, protect the sump and the fuel tank for this reason. They are generally 'big and beefy' and, as one navigator put it, strong enough to stay intact after being hit by a significant

lump of granite at over 100kph. Imagine firing a boulder at a metal plate at that sort of speed, and you get a picture of what the guard has to withstand. It's also worth armouring all the underbody lines, replacing any rubber hoses with braided alternatives. Car with sump and tank guard,

rollcage, 4-point harnesses, plumbed-in extinguisher system, cut-off switch, competition seats: all complying with MSA regulations.

Other basic equipment includes:
Club membership card.
Stage rally driver's licence (BARS).
Navigator with non-race national B

Mini hits land mine! Some British road reallies are rougher than stages. (Courtesy Andy Manston)

licence.
Helmets (for both crew).
Flame retardant overalls (for both crew).
It's also be worth considering an in-helmet intercom system.

PERSONAL EXPERIENCE

When I set out to write a guide to motorsport I knew that, for it to be of most use, I'd have to compete in all the different disciplines included. I set out at the start of the 2002 season with that in mind, and had a long-term project in the form of a shell that I hoped to build to stage rally specification.

However, I am a motorsport addict on a student budget. The cost of regular participation in other disciplines (and regular trips to the bar) meant that the rally car fell behind schedule and is still awaiting completion. So, as I needed to

compete I looked around for a drive. Understandably, no-one I knew wanted to lend an expensive rally car to a complete novice.

As an alternative I asked Sevenoaks and District Motor Club competition secretary, Mark Dawson, to write a version of his account of a single venue rally that he recently co-drove on. Mark co-drive for 1997 ANCRO British champion, Daren Hall, in Daren's ex works Nissan Sunny GTi, a car formerly driven by current WRC star, Alister McRae. Daren has been away from rallying for a while as he can't afford to compete at the level he wants, which is a shame because he is perhaps one of the most talented drivers I know, and deserves a drive in a good series.

Our intrepid duo had entered the Spotted Dick and Custard (don't ask) stages rally, which is a single venue event held at the Longcross vehicle proving grounds in Surrey. The

proving grounds comprise a banked, high speed oval circuit, one side of which has a slight dogleg. Inside the outer high speed ring is a handling course designed to test vehicles to the limit. With its many changes in gradient and direction, the section has been nicknamed the snake. In the centre of the venue is a set of test hills or tank ramps of four hills, each one steeper than the next. Cars take off on the way down and on the way up. At the base of the hills the cars come crashing down on their sump guards, the suspension travelling through its entire movement in a few seconds.

The rally consisted of eight stages, all using different combinations of the venue's extensive tarmac roads. I was marshalling on the ramps throughout. Mark seemed to be enjoying himself and gave us all a wave on his way round. I'll let him take up the story:

Now, how's it supposed to go? - 5,4,3,2,1, GO - sod it, I forgot the stopwatch!! I really don't know why I wore that thing around my neck, I kept forgetting to press the buttons when it mattered. I am, of course, talking about my co-driving exploits on the Spotted Dick.

Mine and Daren's weekend began with setting up on the Saturday, which at least gave us some idea of the layout of the stages. Unfair advantage, I hear you cry, not so; Daren hadn't driven there before, unlike a good proportion of the entry who knew just where Longcross could bite the unwary. The car was also new to him, as was left hand drive, so there!

7am Sunday we waited at the main gates with what seemed like the entire field. Once in, car unloaded, trailer parked, noise passed, scrutineering passed, documents done, it was nearly time for the off. Daren had already stressed how important it was to be quick, straight out of the box. As some competitors take a couple of stages to really get going, this is where we could get an early advantage. All 8 stages were each around 6 miles in length and our SS1 time was pretty good at 4.27, quicker than Dave Jacobs in the MG Metro 6R4, amongst others. That was despite a few missed/crunched gears due to not knowing the car.

SS2 was a re-run of SS1 and we expected - as you do - to go faster second time around. However, on exiting a long right entry chicane (can't think of a better way of describing it!) where the section of road known as the snake joins back up with the outer track, I heard a bang, the car started slewing a bit, and Daren shouted "driveshaft" over the intercom. Bugger, that was probably our biggest concern, we had a spare, but would we make it back with probably about 4 miles still to drive? The fact we did

When this Talbot lands it will most likely do so on its sump guard, without which there would be a hole in the sump, oil on the stage and a dead Talbot engine. (Courtesy Andy Manston)

make it back with a time only 17 seconds slower than SS1 is a testament to the strength and tightness of the diff. Fortunately, we would have nearly an hour in service to effect a remedy. The car was up in the air, wheels off, and I immediately noticed that all six bolts which should be securing the inner CV to the drive flange were hanging out … that'll be the problem, then. Some of the bolts were obviously bent by the force of the diff trying to turn at one speed whilst the wheel wanted to do something else. We had a spare shaft and bolts which were pre-drilled for lockwire. There was no damage to the CV and so we were able to bolt it all back together, finishing off with some lockwire for good measure. Better

check the other side as well, and yep, they were all loose, at least half a turn on them. That side's bolts weren't drilled for wiring them so we decided that it would be wise to check them after every stage.

SS3 and 4 both went okay; a few more missed gears with the occasional over-rev: the Japanese build their engines well! I think it was on SS4 that we caught and passed Terry Luckings in his Golf. I'm frantically shouting at Daren "Go on, up the inside, he's giving you room." Daren's already flat and going for the gap but we were going the long way round on the dusty line and the car was understeering, but we made it.

SS5 and 6 were the first of the stages to run in the reverse direction

**English weather gives every possible scenario - from desert style dust clouds to Scandinavian winter wastelands.
(Courtesy Andy Manston)**

so we would be launching off the top of the tank hill, another new experience, best to play safe with that one and just drop a gear and dab the brakes at the top. Also, these two stages had the longest section of flat-out, at least half a mile long and we were peaking in sixth after about a quarter of a mile. The gearing on the car is set for the forests with about 100mph at 7200rpm. Still more gearbox/operator maladies, Daren was getting peed off at himself by now but

also more determined that he would get one stage together perfectly. We were improving our times on the second runs through the stages, which was the main thing, and were 9 seconds quicker through SS6 than SS5.

Two more stages to go and the long blat of the previous stages was cut out, luckily, that was costing a bit of time. SS7 time was 6.17; I jokingly said to Daren, "Right, I want 7 seconds off next time." Guess what

our SS8 time was? yep, 6.10, and that last stage went beautifully, no missed gears. Sitting in the car I was very much aware of the increased urgency, it just felt more flowing and fast.

A quick look at the results confirmed that we had finished 1st in class and 5th overall, very pleasing for both of us, I can tell you. Life is full of 'if onlys' and 'what ifs' but if only we hadn't had that shaft problem, 3rd might have been on the cards!

Rallying advice

"Try to be quick out of the box; many crews take a couple of stages to get up to speed."

"Try a small, single venue rally before going for it on a multi-venue forest rally."

"Work out a system that both you and your co-driver are happy with for navigation on both road sections and stages."

"Bear in mind that most rallies have at least 50 competitive stage miles; make sure the car will last."

"Get familiar with the mechanical workings of your car, it could be the difference between victory and retirement."

"Make sure the car has a valid MoT, and valid tax and insurance."

"On road sections be aware that ALL usual road traffic regulations apply and sensible behaviour is a must."

"Marshalling is a good way to learn."

"Back off a little before yumps."

Chapter 10
Road rallying

In Wales road rallying is a spectator sport. (Courtesy Andy Manston)

Spotlights are a common addition to many road rally cars, as well as sump guards, both of which can be seen on this Peugeot. (Courtesy Andy Manston)

The tight, twisting, narrow country lanes of rural Britain are almost made for competition motoring. The challenge they offer drivers is incredible, and even more so for navigators because of their winding and interconnecting nature. Sometimes, a friendly farmer will offer up his farm tracks to make things even more exciting. Hours and hours of competition throughout the night provide, perhaps, the best value for money in modern motorsport.

Okay, some basic points about road rallying. They're run on open, public roads; they're not races; they're not illegal; a totally standard car can be used to compete in; the most powerful car is not the best - and, yes they are rather fun!

On a road rally, every car carries a crew comprising a driver and a navigator. The navigator is given a set of directions, written in various forms, which he then plots on an ordinance survey 1:50000 map. The route will almost certainly consist of tight, narrow, winding country lanes that will guarantee a challenging drive.

The object of a road rally is to follow the correct route and keep to the allotted time schedule, arriving at checkpoints precisely on time. Entries are scored on how close they are to the specified arrival time and, more importantly, how well they follow the route. Arriving too early at a control or checkpoint will cost many points in the final scoring, as will not following the correct route.

The route is split into sections, or stages, at the start and finish of each there is a checkpoint where arrival and departure times are recorded. Along the sections there are boards with codes on them that the navigator must record in order to prove that the correct route is followed.

The easiest way to get your head round all the many and various quirks of this sport is just to get out there and compete, you'll pick it up in no time!

A note on 12-car rallies

A good and cheap way to start is with 12-car rallies, which local motor clubs run on short local routes. These mini rallies have a maximum entry of 12 cars (hence the name). 12 cars run to exactly the same regulations and system as a full road rally, but the rally is far shorter - about two hours as opposed to the seven or eight hour

Escorts are not the only Fords on road rallies.
(Courtesy Andy Manston)

Don't bother washing your car before a rally.
(Courtesy Andy Manston)

Rally cars can take some punishment on some of Britain's most
challenging roads - and off them, too. (Courtesy Andy Manston)

There are times when a driver has cause to doubt his navigator.
(Courtesy Andy Manston)

marathons of fullscale road rallies - and entry fees are much, much lower.

THE CAR

Road rally cars vary quite a lot in levels of preparation. Long gone are the days of the super-fast, specialised road rally cars; today's cars are mostly lightly modified shopping runarounds.

The thing about road rallying is that the car is not as important as the crew. Many seasoned road rally crews claim, in fact, that the car's performance has no importance at all: this is wrong; it is of significance. A standard road car can compete on most events without any real damage, although often cars are fitted with uprated brakes and suspension, sump guards, competition seats and harnesses, rollcage and various navigation aids, most of which do not give advantages on the rally route. Some things - such as fire extinguishers and first aid kits - are recommended but not essential.

Some very minor things should be checked before a car is entered for a rally.

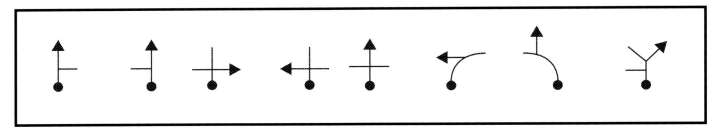

Tulip diagrams

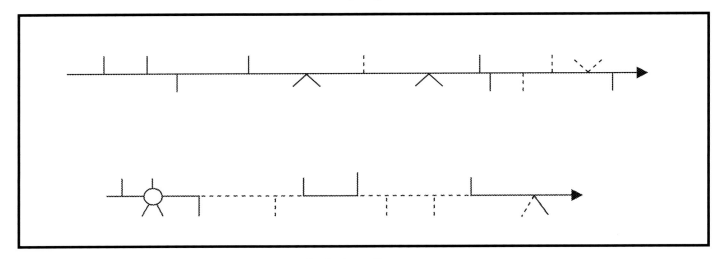

Herringbone diagrams.

Noise

As these events run throughout the night on public roads, and often past houses, every competing car must pass a noise test prior to signing on. The check is carried out using a dB meter, a kind of microphone held at an angle of 45 degrees 500mm from the end of the exhaust. The engine is revved to 4500rpm and the car must not be producing more than 98dB (which is really quite quiet). Try to build up the revs gently and avoid wide throttle openings as this generates extra noise. Ensure that your exhaust system is not 'blowing' and has the standard number of exhaust boxes.

Lighting

All lighting must be fully operational, including indicators and brake lights. Lighting is really quite important as rallies are run in less than ideal conditions, often fog and heavy rain.

Most competitiors use extra lighting. Current regulations allow four forward facing lamps of greater than 21 watts, including headlights. This usually means that cars have standard headlights and a pair of rallying spotlights or twin headlamps.

Bodywork

All bodywork must all be the same colour with no primer showing. Wheelarch extensions are not permitted unless fitted originally. Signwriting is banned and has been since the big changes of 1988.

BASIC GUIDE TO NAVIGATION

Road rally navigation is the reason that so many WRC navigators are British (or should that be Welsh?); it's an archaic system developed over many years to confuse people. But no more, as here's a basic guide to the most common types that you will encounter, together with a few examples of real novice navigation clues as used on the 2002 Kent Rally.

Map references

Six figure references (e.g. 123654), with some fractions to help (e.g. 123.5). You should have come across these, but remember 'along, then up' i.e. the first three numbers measure left

14/2/02

Kent Rally 2002   **Route Card 1**   **Sevenoaks & DMC Ltd**
Issued at **MTC1   at**   **MTC1 to TC2**

CRO
Using the map included with the final instructions join map 188 a 450544$\frac{1}{2}$ then to TC2
which is where the yellow road goes under the M25.

TC2   **WNW   466$\frac{1}{2}$ 557$\frac{1}{2}$ ESE**   *NOVICE*

Time allowed   4 Mins

Kent Rally 2002   **Route Card 2**   **Sevenoaks & DMC Ltd**
Issued at   TC2   **WNW   466$\frac{1}{2}$ 557$\frac{1}{2}$ ESE**   TC2 to TC3

CRO - Spot heights & map symbols
93 191 235 **art**
Please treat Brasted and Brasted Chart very quietly.

TC3   **SW   474$\frac{1}{2}$ 535 NE**   *NOVICE*

Time allowed   7 Mins

Kent Rally 2002   **Route Card 3**   **Sevenoaks & DMC Ltd**
Issued at   TC3   **SW   474$\frac{1}{2}$ 535 NE**   TC3 to TC4

CRO - Map symbols, glid lines & spot heights
Phi 48 53 178 53 49 53 **<** 53 194 53 50 54 134 112

TC4   **SSW   506 548$\frac{1}{2}$ NNE**   *NOVICE*

Time allowed   8 Mins

Kent Rally 2002   **Route Card 4**   **Sevenoaks & DMC Ltd**
Issued at   TC4   **SSW   506 548$\frac{1}{2}$ NNE**   TC4 to TC5

CRO - depart junctions
ESE   SE   SSW   WSW   WNW

TC5   **E   516 524$\frac{1}{2}$ W**   *NOVICE*

Time allowed   5 Mins

Kent rally navigation.

SPEEDPRO SERIES

14/2/02

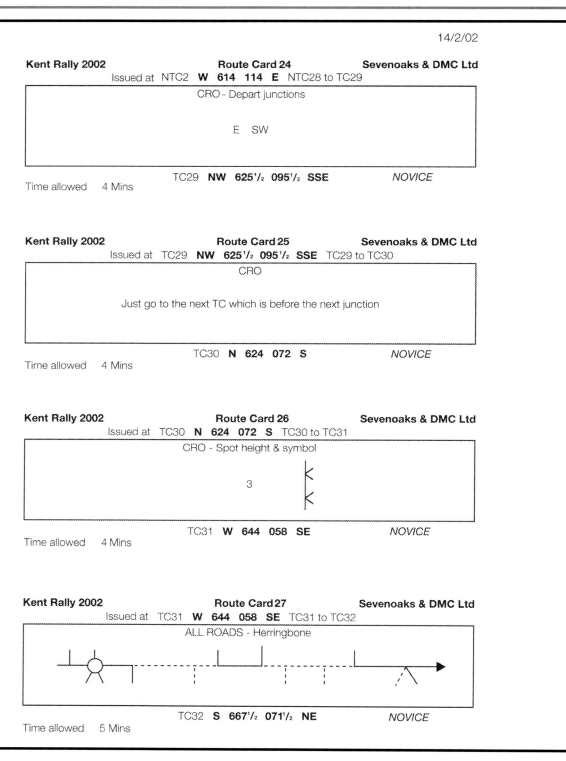

Kent rally navigation.

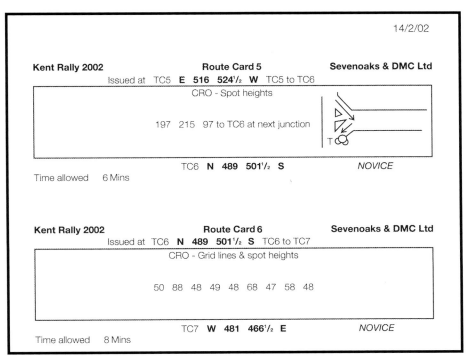

14/2/02

Kent Rally 2002	Route Card 5	Sevenoaks & DMC Ltd

Issued at TC5 **E 516 524½ W** TC5 to TC6

CRO - Spot heights

197 215 97 to TC6 at next junction

TC6 **N 489 501½ S**   *NOVICE*

Time allowed   6 Mins

Kent Rally 2002	Route Card 6	Sevenoaks & DMC Ltd

Issued at TC6 **N 489 501½ S** TC6 to TC7

CRO - Grid lines & spot heights

50 88 48 49 48 68 47 58 48

TC7 **W 481 466½ E**   *NOVICE*

Time allowed   8 Mins

Kent rally navigation.

to right (Eastings) and the next three measure up (Northings). They may well have the direction of approach and departure added thus, ESE123654NW - ESE is the direction from which that map reference is approached and NW is the direction of departure.

Tulip diagrams

This pictographic form of giving directions originated on the Dutch Tulip Rally and first hit the UK rally scene on the 1959 RAC Rally. It's a fairly simple method of depicting junctions. The blob shows the direction of approach and the arrowhead the direction of departure. The shape of the tulip is not always representative of the shape of the junction.

Herring-bones

So called because they look like a fish backbone (well, sort of). The arrowhead depicts the direction of travel. The straight line is the route to follow and the line either side are roads to be ignored. This does not mean that the route is straight or that you never turn off the road that you are on. A line to the left (A) means ignore a road to the left, which can mean just that, or it may mean turn right at a T-junction. Two lines to the right at one point (B) usually mean turn left at crossroads, but may also mean there are two side roads to the right at the same time.

Grid lines

26 53 27 28 29 30 31 53 32 33 34 35

A fairly simple method, the lines already referred to as Eastings and Northings are also known as grid lines and are used for navigation in the same way as other numeric navigation. You will be expected to cross the grid lines in the order given. The above sequence is on map 187

and is, in fact, the eastbound route of the M25 between junctions 8 and 6.

Spot heights

Scattered over the map are numbers in black with small dots next to them - these are spot heights. They give the height in metres of that point above sea level. Many, but not all, of these have dots on roads and it is these that we are interested in. A string of these numbers is often used to define the route. The only spot heights which count are those whose dot falls on a road (including whites). If you look at the spot height 215 in grid square 6260 (on map 188) left of Trottiscliffe, you see that the dot is touching, but not on the road - this shouldn't be used to define a route along that road. The spot height 143 in grid square 6454 south of Mereworth Woods is ideal; the dot is right in the middle of the junction of the B road and the yellow road.

Symbols

These are letters, symbols, etc., for various things - such as churches or an ETL which exist along the route.

Departs

Simply, the compass bearing (N SE NW, etc) giving the direction of departure from junctions.

BASIC EQUIPMENT

Standard road car.
Navigator.
Club membership cards.
National B non-race licence (unless you enter as a clubman).
OS landranger maps.
A roamer.
Map board.
Navigation light.
Torch.

A car can - and probably will - get very, very dirty, as the driver of this Vauxhall discovered. (Courtesy Andy Manston)

PERSONAL EXPERIENCE

Road rallying had always been a bit of an enigma to me. I'd done scatters before, but never a 12-car or road rally; they were a totally different matter and I did not fully understand the rules. It was with this very much in mind that I picked up my friend, Oli North, from a damp train station somewhere in suburbia. We were both about to set off into the unknown.

We had entered my totally standard (and rather aged) road car on the 2002 Kent Rally. Our preparations for this event consisted only of running over how the different types of navigation worked, and making sure that the tyre pressures were correct.

After picking our way through suburbia for around twenty minutes we reached the noise test location - layby on the A25. A funny-looking bloke holding a funny-looking piece of equipment, which resembled a television microphone taped to a stick and wired to a pocket calculator, approached the car. He asked me to rev the engine to 4500rpm and then pointed the stick in the general direction of the exhaust pipe. "Fine!" he shouted and gave Oli a piece of paper which instructed us to continue to the start venue where our car would be scrutineered.

At scrutineering the negative battery terminal was found to be lacking some yellow tape, which was soon supplied. After scrutineering was a competitor briefing, followed closely by a novices' briefing. The first briefing stated where the quiet zones were, how to behave in them (dipped beams, low gear, minimum tyre noise, etc.,) and other basics such as that. The novices' briefing ran through some of the types of navigation that would be encountered during the rally, and how and when to cut route. After this there was quite a long wait before the start at one minute past midnight.

Road rally glossary of terms

Road rally crews and organisers have, over the years, built up a language of their own, quite separate from the rest of the motorsport community. Most of it is in the form of obscure abbreviations and there follows a selection of the more common ones you may encounter. It seems, at first glance, to be a fairly daunting task to learn and understand all of these terms, but in competition it's picked up without even trying. Every now and again some less well-known jargon creeps in and catches out experienced crews, never mind novices. It may be useful to keep this list to hand when on an event just in case ...

AR	All roads: this means the navigation includes every dirt track and driveway, as well as normal roads.
B	Black, Brown or Blue.
BOAT	Byway open to all traffic.
Code board	A board with a code or numbers on that must be recorded.
Coloured roads	Roads shown on the OS map in Yellow, Orange, Red, Green or Blue.
CRO	Coloured roads only.
CTC	Competitive time control (same as TC).
Delta	Long way round triangle (see 'how to' section).
D	Down, generally a < or > symbol on the map.
Dip	Dipped headlights only can be used when you see this.
DPH	Distance on the public highway, do not count distance from whites or public paths.
DSO	Driving standards observer.
E	Even.
ETL	Electricity/transmission line.
TL	Turn left or transmission line.
FL	Fork left (take the left fork) or flat-out left hander.
Foto	Smile!
FP	Public footpath.
FR	Fork right or flat-out left hander.
GL	Grid line.
GS	Grid square.
GW	Give way.
H	Horizontal (in reference to a grid line).
ITC	Intermediate time control.
IGR	Ignore gated roads.
LWR	Long way round, similar to Delta (see 'how to' section).
ML	Miss left (hand turn).
MTC	Main time control.
MR	Miss right or map reference.
MUW	May use whites.
NAM	Not as map.
NTC	Neutral time control.
O	Odd.
OTL	Over total lateness.
PC	Passage check.
PR	Public relations - informing locals of the rally route.
Q	Quiet zone; extinguish spotlights and try to keep engine and tyre noise to a minimum.
Route check	See code board.

(continued overleaf –)

(continued from previous page)

RTC	Regularity time control (very rare).
RUPP	Road uses public path.
SC	Secret check.
SH	Spot height.
SL	Slot left.
Slot	Turn or road.
SO	Straight on or straight over.
SOX	Straight on at crossroads.
SR	Slot right.
STC	Standard time control (same as TC).
SWR	Short way round the opposite of Delta (see 'how to' section).
TC	Time control.
TTC	Transport time control.
TL	Turn left.
TP	Triangulation post.
TR	Turn right.
U	Up or under.
V	Vertical (in reference to a grid line).
XR	Crossroads.
VQ	Very quiet zone; treat it as if driving through a speed camera.
WRI	White roads included/ignored (ask organiser which).
WUW	Will use white roads.
Y	Yellow: minor road depicted in yellow on an OS map.

We used this time to mark up our two OS maps, which involved finding all the blue grid numbers and going over them in black ink, and locating all of the many hundreds of spot heights and highlighting them in Day-Glow yellow. We did this so that these two crucial things could be found in a hurry in the dark.

And then the room slowly started to empty as the clock ticked past midnight. The cars left a minute apart and, as we were car 27, we were due to start at 28 minutes past twelve. With fifteen minutes to go we gathered our things together and headed out into the freezing cold night.

I started the engine and let it tick over for a while to get properly warm. Two rally plates were fixed to the car - one on the left rear window and one on the rear window - and, after a final checkover, we joined the back of the

queue of cars waiting to start. Whilst waiting in line Oli was given the 45 envelopes containing the route cards. Each envelope had a TC (time control or checkpoint) number at which we were supposed to open it.

One by one the cars drove away into the gloom. Our turn came and we were off! Oli was a bit caught out by the first junction and we missed it; realising our error almost instantly we turned around and didn't lose too much time.

A few stages in I got on the tail of a fast Vauxhall that was running in our class and tried to keep up with him - big mistake. The road dropped down to a 90 degree left hander then proceeded over a narrow bridge. I fought for control and just managed to get it onto the bridge. That woke us up.

The rally weaved its sinuous way

for three hours through TC and NTC, up hill and down along the narrow lanes that cover Kent and Sussex like the lines on a crazy paved driveway, until we reached the English Channel, and our fuel stop. The fuel stop gave us a much needed rest; I got out of the car, nearly at breaking point and ready to give up through tiredness. A couple of cans of an energy drink helped a little but not much: if I'd known what was to come I almost certainly would have quit there and then. Fortunately I didn't. Three-and-a-half hours more driving and we encountered fog, black ice, flooded roads, getting lost, clutch problems and countless more code boards and TCs, but these obstacles were all nothing on Pevensey Levels. The Levels came instantly after the fuel halt, roads that cover the flat, featureless landscape, twisting and turning between huge ditches; difficult to drive in good conditions. Nightime, fog rolling in off the sea and icy roads, all combined to make the driving treacherous. We picked our way through very carefully and lost a fair bit of time, as did almost everyone.

By the time we got back on to better lanes I was totally disorientated and getting very tired. For the next hour we lost around a minute per stage and were forced to cut route a couple of times to avoid going OTL (outside total lateness - end of rally). With two hours' driving left to go, I got a second wind and we got going again.

As dawn started to break we were on roads I knew and I was able to up our tempo quite a bit. We finally reached the final TC, tired, hungry and happy in the knowledge that we had managed to finish. With around seven hours of hard motoring behind us, we headed off to a pub with all the other finishers in search of some well-earned breakfast. I can't remember much about the breakfast, though I couldn't eat a lot through sheer tiredness.

We discovered later that the Kent is one of the more gruelling events. It's great fun, though - honestly! We took part in the rally as a one off, a bit of fun, and now we compete in every round of the local championship.

The event after the Kent was shorter and less gruelling, but equally enjoyable and we very nearly won our class! So, you can see that, even though it all seems very confusing and off-putting at the start, it's possible to pick it up rather quickly.

SCATTERS

A cheap and fun way to get into rallying. My first ever motorsport event was a scatter and it was a great way to start.

Scatter rallying is an oddity in motorsport, without a set route, no timing and no emphasis on speed. Checkpoints are randomly placed around a fairly large area, and the winner the crew that visits the most checkpoints within the allowed time. Crews prove they have visited a point by recording some information (which

is specifically asked for on the answer sheet); often the number on a telegraph pole or some information on a sign at the location. On the featured rally, the information required as proof of visiting a check was the name of the manufacturer of a padlock, which had first to be located! I should add that it is generally impossible to visit all of the checkpoints in the given time.

Scatters: personal experience

Apart from a few arrive-and-drive kart races, I had not previously competed in a motorsport event of any kind. Also, having passed my driving test (second attempt) only a few months earlier, I had all the driving talent of a citrus fruit, so - understandably - was a little nervous on the drive down. Sitting next to me was my long-suffering mate, Will, who was to call the shots, map-wise; oh, and he'd never even watched a rally on TV! This really was a first for both of us ...

We arrived at the start venue, a farmhouse pub perched on top of the North Downs just south of London.

Rallying advice
"Road rallying really is a team effort as you have to concentrate under pressure for long periods of time. Make sure you get on with your driver/navigator."
"Do a few 12-cars before going on to a national B event, or some rallies run a clubman's event running behind the national B; start off with that."
"Make sure all the car's lights and systems are working reliably as they'll take some punishment through the night."
"Outright speed does not determine the winner of a rally, so try to follow the correct route, getting all the code boards - missing a board could mean a 30 minute penalty so it's worth spending fifteen minutes looking for it."
"The events take place through the night so you are fighting off tiredness, stimulating drinks such as Red Bull can help. Stay up late the night before the event and spend as much as you can of the next day asleep; natural insomnia helps!"
"Remember that, on the whole, the route is on public roads, so the usual laws apply - including the speed limit!"
"Check the Blue Book to see if your car is eligible to compete; twin cams, for instance, are banned."
"Some events are more damaging to the car than others. The Preston is very rough, for instance; check the regs to see how bad it will be and, if in doubt, ring and ask."
"A roamer is essential."
"Take a plank of wood in case you have to change a wheel on a soft surface."
"Take the time to plot references correctly. With a highlighter pen go over all the spot heights on the map, and go over the grid line numbers with a black pen; it really makes a difference."

A Talbot dropped from a plane into the East Sussex chocolate sauce depository. (Courtesy Andy Manston)

We sat down with the rest of the crews and the organisers, the only thing distinguishing us from regular pub-goers being our alcohol-free drinks.

We paid our entry fee - just five pounds - and when all the competitors were assembled we were given our clue sheets and the clock started. A short dash out to the car was followed by a half-hour sitting puzzling over the clues. Will found a checkpoint that was not too far away and pointed to it on the map, I knew the road it was on well so we shot off to read a public footpath sign that was about three miles away.

The checkpoint sheet asked us to record the total mileage on the sign. It read Biggin Hill one-and-a-half miles, so we jotted that down and headed off in search of more checkpoints that Will had found on the map. For just under two hours we continued through the Kent and Surrey hills, looking for numbers on telegraph poles, counting the number of white stones by the roadside, and similar things that Scatter rallies ask for at checkpoints. At one point we arrived at what we were certain was a checkpoint but which turned out to be the middle of a forest! There was no way we were going to do very well as we were struggling.

After countless phantom checkpoints, country lanes, and attempts to chase other competitors, we noticed that the clock read 22.15. We were due back at the start and finish venue (the aforementioned farmhouse pub) in 15 minutes and were a fair old way away from it. Suddenly, I foolishly realised that, between us and the pub, were the roads I drove every day. I told Will there was no need for directions as I knew these roads quite well. Suffice to say we were only a couple of minutes late and, even though the last crew to arrive, did well for a first attempt, despite finishing last.

We compared notes with the other crews while the organisers worked out the results. One crew, a pair of brothers, had come across a young couple getting up to some motorsport activity of their own at one checkpoint! By the sounds of it, they must have been testing some suspension settings ...

The results completed we discovered we were equal last, but that's what we expected. We scored half points only for the first checkpoint we visited (the footpath sign) as, apparently, mileages on both sides of the sign were required. Oh well ... It was great fun and, since that event, I have competed in a few other Scatters and have even run one of my own.

Road rallying - it's a Mini adventure! (Courtesy Andy Manston)

Rallying Escort. (Courtesy Andy Manston)

Sevenoaks and District Motor Club

Welcome to Weald Motor Club's first Scatter of the 2002/03 season. I have tried to provide a challenge for both navigators and drivers by including some of my favourite driving roads and some tricky clues. You'll set off at 20.15 and, as this is a fairly short event, I expect to see you all back by the due time of 22:00. Lateness will be penalised at 5 points per minute. OTL is 22.15. Finish venue is back at the Botley Hill farmhouse.

The map used is 187, all clues plot on post-1995 editions.

I will be looking for accurate answers and will employ negative marking at 5 points per incorrect answer to help prevent cheating by guessing. If you're not sure, leave it blank! Unless stated, numbers on telegraph poles are those in white roundels.
Be aware of speed cameras on the A25 and M25, there is a good fun little jump at 5140 2955.

CRO.
3955 6380.
TZW VQY.
From 5 heading uphill then latvia, russia, lithunania, lichenstien, rwanda, regency, regency, latvia, russia clue is where first foot path arrives from london.
93385.25 x 4.
3585 5250.
Church at 239.
EDGAFHDF.
4430 5985.
OKT QKM.
625 373.
163 at Farleigh.
592 371.
5800 3770.
34 80 57 15.
35805765.
F3D5 D3B5.
From 3, head south, MR, ML (NAM), MR, MR, TL, 245, 265, TR, ML, MR, TL, TR, follow A25 through Godstone to 103 then ML, ML, XR. Clue is at square left.
516301.
x 2 XUUYVR.
511 347.
5025035300.
Catch the train from Redhill bound for Tonbridge. Wait until the train has gone over eleven bridges and under three, through a tunnel and a pair of stations. As soon as the train passes under the fourth pull the cord and scramble up the bank to the nearest junction.
Where rail passes above rail and road crosses above both.
501 414.
WUW Burger King at Clacket Lane.

What characters have been removed from the red tag?
Total mileage on FP sign.
What's the name of the Path?
Phone number of Woodland trust (sign in CP).
Where was the padlock on the gates made?
Service times on the last Sunday of each month.
What diameter is the gas pipeline (stated on small sign)?
Total FP mileage on sign.
What is the name of this walk?
What number is painted on the circular concrete block?
What diameter is the gas pipeline (not the same as 7)?
What is written on the white stone post?
Manufacturers of both padlocks?
How much is the muck?
What is the name of the lock-up garage?
Name of cottage?
What are the stated destinations of cycle route 21?
Number on telegraph pole?
Colour of box on gates?
What numbers are on the fire hydrant sign?
Numbers on telegraph pole?
What is the name of the building nearest to the junction?
At what time is the last collection by Consignia Monday-Friday?
Numbers on telegraph pole.
How much is a triple cheeseburger?

Clue sheet for a 'Scatter' rally giving the locations of the checkpoints. It is given out to competitors at the start of the allowed time.

Chapter 11
Speed events

Hillclimbing in Kent. No walking boots or ramblers here! (Courtesy Colin Shipway)

All were surprised at the performance put in by this unexpected entry at a Sprint on an Essex Airfield. (No, not the car!) (Courtesy Colin Shipway)

The war left many airfields for Sprints to be held on, although often they turn out to be glorified high speed Autotests. (Courtesy Colin Shipway)

The narrow, flowing drives of country houses, the wide, bleak featureless expanses of old airfields, and the swooping tarmac of race circuits all, with varying frequency, lend themselves to the competitive world of speed events.

Sprinting and Hillclimbing are the two main types of speed event, but are basically the same thing. Cars compete singly against the clock and the best time wins. There are no professionals but, in the British championship, the top cars can out-accelerate a modern Grand Prix car. The cars are as highly tuned and nearly as hi-tech as any manufactured by Williams, Ferrari or McLaren for the Formula One World Championship. On the same event, however, a number of unmodified hatchbacks of the type seen, on the side of the road, for sale for a few hundred pounds are forced up the hill by drivers without the budget or inclination to run a big-engined special. In-between these two extremes exists an amazing range of machinery.

HISTORY

Arriving in Bexhill-on-Sea by road there are signs proclaiming this town on the Sussex coast to be the birthplace of British motorsport. These signs are referring to the Bexhill Speed Trials of 1902 but, in reality, the Bexhill event was not the beginning of British motorsport, or even the beginning of Speed events.

Timed speed hillclimbs are - along with much of motorsport - a French invention, the first event taking place at Chanteloup in 1898. Perhaps the Automobile Club of Great Britain and Ireland (forerunner of the RAC) took notice of this as, the following year, it included a timed run up Petersham Hill in Richmond as part of its General Efficiency trials; there was also a 1.5 mile speed trial on a straight road. Both the hillclimb and the speed trial took place on open public roads, although the 12mph speed limit was never really under threat as the cars of

Cars of any age can take part in speed events. (Courtesy Colin Shipway)

the day were not that fast.

The pioneering automotive sportsman, S. F. Edge, proposed a sporting speed hillclimb in the North Downs. More of the proving trials, such as the pair of events in 1899, took place, many on public roads and some at illegal speeds. In the summer of 1900, two events of the type proposed by S .F. Edge took place with some success.

In 1901, a number of clubs ran hillclimb events with varying degrees of success. 1902 brought the so-called 'birth' I mentioned earlier at Bexhill; the seafront speed trial along the De la Warr-prepared parade attracted international entries and really established speed as a discipline.

There were problems with the events taking place on the public road as the 12mph speed limit was enforced. A venue on private ground was found at Shelsley Walsh in

Oh yes you can! This Bentley is standard production. I thought this was more interesting than the Peugeot 205 that I was going to illustrate here. (Courtesy Colin Shipway)

The McCoy 'North Kent Special' runs in the kit car class.

Worcestershire, and, on August 12th 1905, the world's longest-serving motorsport venue held its first meeting. (Shelsley Walsh is still in use today.)

The opening of Brooklands in 1907 had a detrimental affect on speed events, which began to wane in popularity as competitors drifted in the direction of the Surrey autodrome. There was still good competition to be had in these bleak times, however, especially at northern venues and Shelsley Walsh. The cars were improving vastly (the positive side-effect of Brooklands) with higher-revving engines and increased speed.

The sport seemed to be freeing itself from the mire in which it was stuck just in time for the outbreak of World War One. By the start of the hostilities cars were sleeker and even faster than ever before, and many were capable of breaking today's motorway speed limit.

It's been said that the period following the first war could be tagged the 'adolescence of speed.' Ever-increasing speeds were attracting spectators to public road events which were, strictly speaking, illegal.

In 1919, Middlesex AC restarted speed competition officially by running an event at Hand Post Hill. There were very few events that year as the world struggled to its feet after years of conflict. The speed scene soon got back into stride in a big way and the calendar swelled with numerous events, many clashing. The sport became more and more popular; an event at Thundersley in Essex attracted 600 entries (although this was partially due to cars being double-entered). The meeting was chaotic but must have been a sight to see.

Public road events were still occurring in 1925, but the motoring press was spreading doom and gloom

All sorts of Exotica run alongside mundane everyday cars. (Courtesy Colin Shipway)

Trying hard. (Courtesy Colin Shipway)

Modified production Renault. (Courtesy Colin Shipway)

British motorsport is often wet ... (Courtesy Colin Shipway)

Metro 6R4 at Crystal Palace. (Courtesy Colin Shipway)

about speed events. The end finally came in April of that year. The RAC, fearing the sport would be the target of much hostility, banned the issue of permits for speed events run on the public road. This ban meant that events could only be held at Shelsley Walsh.

This situation continued until 1937 when a new hill at Prescott was found and the Bugatti Owners Club started preparing it for competition events.

The one venue sport was extremely popular and the main event became something of a motoring institution. Events took place on an irregular basis at other venues, too. Events drew huge spectator crowds in the 1930s and often over two hundred entries. The prize for BTD had grown to two hundred and fifty pounds by 1935, a significant sum. The venue itself was developing, too, with better facilities and spectator areas appearing every year.

In 1936 the Germans arrived with the Silver Arrows, or one, anyway. Hans Stuck came to Shelsley for the second year running, this time in the short chassis V16 Auto Union, a simply astonishing car. However, the German's car was not best suited to a soggy Worcestershire and failed to break the course record.

From 1937 the sport acquired a number of new venues - as already mentioned, the most notable of which was Prescott - and looked set to grow in a major way. Once again, unfortunately, world war brought motorsport to a complete halt.

The Second World War left Europe in ruins and short of just about everything, including petrol. New tyres were scarce to the point of non-existence. However, the massive air campaign had left Britain covered in airfields which had lots of sealed roads and runways. Motor racing was in a bad way as the circuits at Brooklands, Donington and Crystal Palace were

totally out of action for at least the near future.

These problems were not felt so keenly in the speed world where less fuel was used and tyres were able to endure more events. The venues were available, too, with Shelsley Walsh running in 1946, along with the first of the airfield sprints.

The RAC decided that a national hillclimb championship was in order. The larger meetings were attracting great entries, with all the pre-war racers that could be mustered wheeled out to compete. Raymond Mays won the inaugural British championship in 1947.

The sport grew in the postwar era with the 500 movement of the 1950s, as cash-strapped competitors built 500cc racers. This was the era of the Cooper-Jap as the tiny cars won every championship from 1951 to 1961. Venues were becoming more numerous and Prescott was extended.

The little Coopers were finally

The unique SRG1 single-seater. (Courtesy Colin Shipway)

Motorcycle-engined cars are often very quick. (Courtesy Colin Shipway)

A good start is crucial.

eclipsed as the advances in technology made them obsolete. The sixties witnessed the continuation of new venues and the birth of the ever-present Mini.

In recent years sprinting and hillclimbing has lost many venues but is still a strong and healthy sport, with events taking place most weekends throughout the season.

CAR - NORMAL CLASSES

Speed classes vary somewhat from region to region, although most of Southern England runs the same regulations. At the time of writing, however, the class structure of the South West varied from the rest of the country. The following is a rough guide to what you might expect. (Many of these classes are often sub-divided into engine size and chassis type.)

Road saloons & sports cars

In some areas these classes cater for standard cars only, in others, modified cars are run together with standard cars. In both cases the cars must have current tax and MoT, be insured for use on the public highway, and in a road legal condition. Sometimes, small sports cars are run in this class.

Road-going kit & replica cars

These classes are usually full of Lotus 7 derivatives such as the Caterham and Westfield, and often cars like the Lotus Elise and Exige run in this class. All cars must be licensed for road use and must compete in a road legal condition.

Modified production cars

Mod prod cars result in highly varied classes, and are often contenders for outright event wins. Generally based on production cars, mod prods are often highly tuned, supercharged beasts. These cars are my favourite to watch during speed events as no two are the same and all are super-impressive. Chevette HSRs and early Escorts are commonplace.

Sports libre cars

Defined by the MSA as any of the following: special saloons, sports racing cars, hillclimb supersports chassis cars, group B rally cars, GT1 sports cars, world rally cars. Most events include sports libre cars of some description, most commonly group B and world rally cars. Metro 6R4s are amazingly common on sprints.

Single-seaters

Open-wheeled classes for purpose-built racing cars. Everything from motorcycle-engined specials to grand prix cars to the purpose-built hillclimbers of the British championship run in these classes. This is possibly the most technologically interesting class with some mind-boggling, one-off specials.

BASIC EQUIPMENT

National B non-race licence.
For the car the following are recommended: rollcage, competition seats, hand-held extinguisher, cut-off switch.
Helmet.
Overalls.
Valid club membership card.
You may need to produce an MoT, insurance and ownership documents.

PERSONAL EXPERIENCE

I drove my first race at the Lydden motor circuit (as I describe elsewhere within these pages) and now I was heading back to what, in my opinion, is Kent's best circuit for my first speed event, Rochester Motor Club's Lydden sprint.

It was very wet and foggy, and really quite early in the morning, when I set off down the A2. The earlier than normal start was due to the event having to finish at lunchtime, when the

Speed events always provide a very mixed bag of entries, as pretty much any car can take part. (Courtesy Colin Shipway)

South East Motorsport Enthusiasts Club (SEMSEC) was running a race meeting. This meant that the only other people on the old Roman Road that runs from London to Dover were competitors. I passed quite a few I knew from other events where I had marshalled. Some were taking their competition cars to the track on trailers and others - like me - were driving there.

I was entered for the lowest class, which had simple entry requirements: standard road cars of any engine size which have a value of less than £3000. Amazingly, the class had only one other entry. (I later found out that quite a few other eligible cars had entered higher classes as the championship points were better.) The other entry was a slightly tatty BMW 318; the two of us were probably the most unlikely looking pair ever to grace a race circuit!

Before I went to scrutineering I had to sign on. As I was entered in a standard production class I had to produce the registration document, MoT and insurance certificate. Being very organised, as usual, I had remembered to bring all of these

things, along with my competition licence, so was not concerned when the secretary of the meeting checked through my documents. Disaster struck when the nice lady from SEMSEC pointed out that my insurance had expired. I was furious with myself; I'd picked up an old certificate, so much for being very organised. The lack of a valid insurance certificate forced me to run in a non-road-going class with cars that were specially prepared for sprinting. I stood no chance.

I voiced my protests but rules are rules and I couldn't challenge this decision. Rather than running second on the road with all the other production cars, I was to run later than my original slot, with the super-powerful and fast cars that were in my new class. At this point I had to visit the start line marshals and explain that, as I would be running much slower than everyone else in my class, a bigger than normal gap should be left before the next car followed me out. They agreed and I joined the queue of cars waiting in the holding area.

In the Steve McQueen film *Le*

Mans, there's a scene where the drivers are waiting for the race to start and the tension - even for the viewer - is tremendous. I found out how that felt now. The cars in front of me left one by one and my nervousness grew. Soon, there was just a Lotus in front of me, the vicious burble of its engine drowning out the gentle rattle of my own. I switched mine off, and opened the window a bit as I was getting quite warm. Soon, the rear wheels of the Lotus spun as it struggled to get away from the line on the slippery surface, then it was my turn. I closed the window and, in so doing, closed out the drone of highly-tuned racing engines, and the bustle and noise of the paddock, and got into the right frame of mind.

I switched on the engine and inched forward to the point the marshals indicated. The old heart was pumping by this time, I can tell you. The starting signal was a red light to green light system. The red light came on and I selected first gear and held the car on the clutch; the light turned to green and my left foot came up and my right foot went down at the same time. For the briefest moment the engine hesitated, then, as if pushed from behind, I was off down the track, the engine sounding fantastic.

I braked and turned in for the first curve but oversteered. I applied armfuls of opposite lock but the slide continued, I caught it with the car still travelling down the track but pointing at the grass bank on the inside of the bend. Suddenly, the front wheels gripped and the bonnet shot round back in the right direction. It kept rotating as the rear end came round onto the slippery grass and I found myself staring straight at the marshals' post on the outside of the track. By this point, I had stopped the car and had it nicely parked on the side of the

had a wide smile on my face by the time I passed the chequered flag. My second run came and went and I improved my time, although was still the slowest competitor on track, barring a strangely slow Renault Alpine and a single-seat racing car that had spread its engine over the Kent countryside on its first timed run.

On returning to the paddock I was told that there was time enough to let those who wanted to have another timed run. I was pleased to hear this, but some of the other competitors didn't seem so keen and started to tell me horror stories of how the big accidents always happen on the third run, and how they never do it. In the end only about half the field took up the option of a third run, myself included, although with all those horror stories fresh in my mind I ran a lot slower than I had done previously.

I missed out on all the awards; my fastest time was just over a second slower than that of the BMW which won the budget class I had originally intended to compete in. Even though I was generally out-driven, and my under-powered and ill-handling car was not a patch on the other machinery, I was hooked, and have since acquired a fibreglass chassis two-seater to sprint and hillclimb in.

circuit. The marshal waved to me that the track was clear and off I drove to complete the run.

On returning to the paddock I was expecting a ticking off from the clerk of the course for making such an error. When I got out of the car, however, I was greeted by a spot of banter about being at the wrong

venue for grass track racing, and really felt like one of the sprinting crowd, who push right to the limit.

The track had a dry line by the time I was due to start my timed run. The lights turned green and I was off, charging down the straight towards the scene of my earlier 'moment,' but this time I took the corner a lot easier. I

Speed event advice

"The start is important; get a quick getaway without too much wheelspin."

"Stay cool."

"Make sure you are comfortable in the car and can reach all the controls easily."

"Drive with your head - you'll find it's a lot cheaper than the seat of your pants."

"Have fun and stay out of trouble."

"Look out for flag signals and follow them to the letter; usually only the red is used."

"Note where the finish line is and slow right down after it."

Chapter 12
Student motorsport

The Oxford Brookes University Formula Student car on display at the *Autosport* show.

Student motorsport may sound like an unlikely chapter title for this book but, in fact, it's one of the most significant areas of British amateur motorsport. Cash-strapped students find ways to get their motorsport fix on a regular basis. Most universities and even some colleges have active motor clubs which organise a variety of events, from autotests and road rallies to a British championship.

Student motorsport has some inherent problems which have plagued it since inception: there's no association to enable the students to get together and discuss matters; inter-university rivalry is rife, and there's a high membership turnover as older members leave university and new members join. Many of these problems are not insurmountable, but student apathy and the increasing problem of student debt prevents solutions being sought. Still, every year it somehow seems to come together and, although there's often acrimony, there's always great motorsport, hotly contested in events around the country.

It's not all about driving skill, though, as technical excellence is showcased in the annual Formula Student competition. For part of their degree courses engineering students design and build single-seat racing cars, powered (generally) by a 600cc motorcycle engine, which they then race against each other in an annual competition.

The big problem with student motorsport is that you have to be a student to do it!

HISTORY

The two most famous institutions of education in Britain don't really like each other much, and compete with barely concealed animosity in rowing,

Student motorsport has traditionally been the training ground for stars of the future, such as Richard Seaman. Two such up-and-coming student racers are Spanish F3 star, Emilio D'Villota and Channel Islander, Matt Ford.

rugby, cricket, and - since the 1920s - motorsport.

Cambridge was first off the mark when, in 1902 a Professor Inglis became president of the brand new Cambridge University Automobile Club (CUAC). The club ran with some success for ten years. Oxford was eight years slower getting a club together and somewhat less efficient; the Oxford University Motor Car Club (OUMCC) was unofficially cobbled together in 1910. The Cambridge club was restarted and closed in quick succession when its 1913 revival was brutally halted by the 1914-18 world war, which also put paid to the OUMCC.

By 1922, both clubs were well and truly back with Oxford's club renamed the Oxford University Motor Club (OUMC). In 1923, the first inter-varsity motorsport event took place. Varsity events were not restricted to summer speed events as gruelling trials were held during the winter.

The student scene continued at the same pace as Oxford and Cambridge battled to get one over on the other. More student clubs had started by now with the University of London and London Hospitals Club organising race meetings in the 1930s. The inter-varsity events were attracting some real talent, such as Cambridge undergraduate, Richard Seaman, who won a class in the 1934 event in his MG Magnette and went on to be a works Mercedes grand prix driver. Oxford continued with its identity crisis, changing its name to Oxford University Car Club and then again to Oxford University Motor Drivers Club (OUMDC), which has stuck to this day.

From 1936 the varsity speed events were held just outside Grantham at Syston, and the winter trial events in the Chiltern Hills. The

students managed to run both their speed event and the winter trial in 1939 before hostilities once again broke out on the continent.

After the second World War Oxford and Cambridge continued to dice in their 'Varsity challenges but there were no records available until the early eighties, which saw a revolution in student motorsport, when the universities of Salford, Leeds, Sheffield, Liverpool and Lancaster joined forces to form the Northern Universities Motor Club (NUMC). The aim of the new club was to promote student motorsport and to encourage competition between member institutes.

In 1982 a student called Bill Balme came up with the idea of running a road rally, an autotest and perhaps a PCT as a national competition. Endsleigh university jumped on the bandwagon as the title sponsor and, in the academic year 1982/83, the Endsleigh National Student Motorsport championship was first run. The event ran on a very foggy night and consisted of a road rally and an autotest; the PCT idea, it seems, was abandoned at the planning stage. The final result seems to have been lost in the sands of time.

A year later the event ran again under the command of Leigh Travis of Salford University and was won by a crew from Leeds University. The event ran along similar lines, with the notable addition of a tabletop rally for navigators, until 1987 when the road rally section used an existing event to reduce organisation.

In 1996 a new inter-university championship was formed for the fans of four wheeled sport, although those four wheels were to be quite small. The National University Karting Championship started off as a five round championship, with three

outdoor endurance races, one grand prix format event and one (unpopular) indoor round. The series was an immediate hit and quickly attracted the attention and participation of most of the active student motor clubs. The name soon changed to the Inter-University Karting Championship (IUKC) and the series raced on.

In the USA in the seventies a student engineering competition had begun, the brief of which was to design a racing car from scratch, build it and pit it against other creations from other higher education establishments. Formula SAE - as it was known - became a popular part of engineering degree courses, and the cars increasingly hi-tech.

A British student by the name of Andrew Deakin was studying in the States for twelve months of his engineering degree, and became involved with a Formula SAE team. On his return to the UK he persuaded a somewhat reluctant and doubtful Leeds University (where he was a student) to put together a team to build a car for the annual competition. The project eventually got the green light and Leeds University was the first-ever British institution to build a Formula SAE car.

The car was entered for the 1997 event in Detroit and finished 50th out of 97 entries. Leeds had set a precedent and in 1998 Formula SAE came to the UK as Formula Student. Initially, the number of entries was much lower than that of the US version. A delegation of three American teams made their way to the NEC in Birmingham, where the competition was held, to boost the numbers. They dominated the event with their years of experience. Experience showed its value again when Leeds scooped the best UK entry. Formula Student has become

Formula (Oxford) Brookes Motor Club chairman, Craig Dawson, gets ready in the IUKC paddock at Rye House.

an essential part of the many automotive and mechanical engineering courses offered in the UK.

Meanwhile, back in the land of punting, Pimms and rowing, the new IUKC had sparked an idea and the inaugural inter-varsity kart race was dreamed up. On a cold and rather wet February day at the Hoddeston kart circuit, Oxford University triumphed over Cambridge in the 1999 race. As

kart tracks require more than two teams to run an economical meeting, teams from other institutions were invited for the next year's race, a tradition which continues. Rallying hadn't been neglected, either, as the varsity rally (now a 12-car) runs to this day.

The National Student Championship also still runs with the 2001 event postponed because of the

foot-and-mouth crisis. When the event did finally resume it was not strongly supported, perhaps because it had twice been postponed, and when it did run it clashed with a round of the Southern Road Rally championship (which has quite a few student crews). All that and the fact that it was run in Scotland left it short of southern (*i.e.* English) crews. The event is sure to return with strength one foggy and wet

Inter-varsity karting driver racing into the night.

winter's night in the near future.

PERSONAL EXPERIENCE

For most of these personal experience sections I recount the often-disastrous exploits of my first event of a certain discipline. However, for this section, I'm going to tell you about my experiences in the 2002 Inter-Varsity race at Whilton Mill.

In early 2002 I was a student at Oxford Brookes University, and a very active member of the just one year old Formula Brookes Motor Club. We had been invited to enter the varsity races after the club's strong members' championship, races held at the Oxford Stadium circuit, and its good first showing in the IUKC had come to the attention of CUAC and OUMDC.

Brookes entered four karts, along with teams from Imperial, York and Loughborough (and, of course, Oxford and Cambridge). All-in-all there were thirty two karts, each with a team of around four drivers. The event was a three hour endurance race on the 850 metre national circuit.

After another rather typical drivers' briefing our team headed off to the edge of the pit lane to get itself arranged.

Practice was a frantic half-hour affair with all drivers needing to practice and many learning the circuit for the first time. My turn came as the number 2 Brookes kart swung into the pits and we carried out a practice driver change. I quickly jumped into the driver's seat and, before the previous driver had his feet on the tarmac, was off down the pits to try and learn the circuit and get to know the kart we were racing. I was used to the karts that we had been using in the Oxford-based karting student championship, which were less powerful than the twin-engined karts of the varsity race.

Out of the pits I drove and was soon flat-out on the back straight. Something was wrong, however, as the engines felt very breathless and I was finding it difficult to overcome the grip offered by the tyres. I couldn't fathom the problem and plugged on; the funny thing was that I was running at a reasonable pace. Our quickest driver (unfortunately, not me) managed to get our kart twelfth on the grid. The Brookes plan was to have two karts going all-out for the overall race win, and the other two trying to get a strong top ten finish. Our kart was one of those looking for a top ten finish.

The race got underway and two of the Brookes karts were already challenging for the lead. It was a long race and I had a fairly late stint, so I jumped into my car to grab a burger and a crate of beers for the end of the event - after all, it was a student race! My regular road rally navigator, Oliver North, was driving for the Brookes team, too, and he came along with me to get the beers. We got some funny looks wandering around a supermarket in full race wear!

On returning to the track it was time for my stint; another swift driver change later I was in the thick of the race and running eighth, close behind a slower kart which was not making it easy for me to pass. I spent a fair few laps scrapping with this guy, trading track position corner after corner, eventually passing him flat-out on a corner that I hadn't taken flat-out before. I seemed to be out on my own for most of my stint. I saw one of the faster Brookes karts (which were now holding the first two places) being quite badly held up by a gaggle of slower machines having a huge scrap. All-in-all about seven karts were running in a bunch, having a huge battle and really slowing each other as well as badly hindering the leading Brookes kart at the back that was desperately trying to pass.

I realised that I was going to catch up with the bunch on the fastest part of the track. I got a great run out of the final corner of the lap and was catching the back of the bunch, two of which were trying to pass each other on the straight, and had no idea I was there until I was running abreast with them. I passed the pair of them in a messy move but managed to carry my speed through and onto the tail of the group. Again, my arrival on the scene went unnoticed: it was beginning to feel like I was driving a stealth kart! I overtook the entire group, underbraking into a slow right hand corner with the troubled Brookes kart following me through.

My stint continued for a while after that and I had quite a few hairy moments and some super dices. My team-mates called me in for the end of my stint and, on the approach to the pit, I was unsighted by another kart and nearly stuffed it into the pit wall!

The excitement was building as a few guys cracked open the beers and sat back to watch the rest of the race, confident of a Brookes victory. As the entire race had been a close affair we were pleased to see the second (Imperial) and third placed (Brookes) drivers going at it hammer and tongs. With just a handful of laps to go the Imperial driver made a small error that allowed the Brookes karts to run first and second.

Oxford and Cambridge, neither of which team had been anywhere in the overall standings (but were bitterly contesting the varsity honours), started getting a bit upset at each other's tactics during the course of the event. Then the big problems started as one of Imperial's slower karts deliberately rammed our race leader, forcing both karts into the pits for a safety check. Then, for reasons that have never become clear, our second-placed entry was called in for a safety check with only two laps left in the race. Imperial was gifted the race win. A good event had been spoiled by inter-university rivalry although it was quite nice to see eternal rivals Oxford and Cambridge race as hard as ever.

Chapter 13
Trials

Bill and Liz Bennett in their MG J2 on Mackhouse 2 - part of the Exmoor Clouds trial of 1999. (Courtesy Derek Hibbert)

Mud, hills and funny little cars. The sport of trialling is all about driving as far up a hill as you can. Not just any hill, mind you; the organisers of these events go to great lengths to find the steepest, muddiest hills they can, and to make them that bit harder to climb, they devise tight routes up (and sometimes down at points) the slopes.

Cones or stakes mark out the routes which are numbered 12-0 as the hill ascends. Whichever number the competitor gets to (or, as the MSA puts it: "ceases forward motion"), is the number of points scored, with 12 being very bad and 0, or a 'clean,' as it is known, the best possible. This is one of only a few motorsport

If you go down to the woods today...

disciplines that has no timing element; in trial all that matters is getting up the hill as far as possible.

The cars run from standard hatchbacks and saloons to purpose-built cars that look like they were designed in the 1930s and built in a farmer's shed from old bits of tractor; sort of Heath-Robinson meets Worzel Gummidge (sorry JC, it's a great line!). Trials cars carry two people - the

driver and a 'bouncer.' In trials a 'bouncer' is not a thug in a cheap suit standing at the entrance to a seedy nightclub, but someone who literally bounces around the car, trying to gain extra traction for the driven wheels by their weight.

HISTORY

At the dawn of motoring,

manufacturers pitted their machines against each other's to try and prove their reliability. These events consisted of long runs with onboard observers watching to make sure the vehicles completed the correct course within the time schedule, and without coming to an involuntary halt. Getting to the destination was the important thing rather than the time it took.

Many roads in those early days

Totally standard, everyday cars compete in PCTs.

were built for the horse and cart and were often rough and muddy. Cars were built on large diameter wheels, and high ride heights were the order of the day. The sport was known as mud plugging as often the roads were quagmires. Drivers would deliberately seek out the worst of these roads and see how far they could drive up them before getting stuck. These more difficult roads became known as sections.

Technology improved both cars and roads which meant that steeper hills were used, with the cars starting from stationary and attempting to ascend. Soon, offroad hills were found which were unsurfaced and even harder to climb.

Specialist cars were being built in small numbers. They had great names such as Troll, and competed alongside Austin 7s and Ford 10s. Car technology had progressed to the

extent that the use of offroad hills became more common. Steep farmland and woodland was sought, along with quarries, to provide a challenge.

The cars became more and more specialised over the years and the sporting trials cars of today evolved. Production cars competed on events throughout and still do on PCTs and Classic trials. Interestingly, prewar trials hills (more great names coming

Classic trials are not just for classic cars, though they are a regular sight on all trials, as this nice special proves.

up) such as Beggars Roost and Nailsworth Ladder, are still more than a match for the cars of today.

CAR - NORMAL CLASSES

There are three types of trialling, as follows:

Production car trials

Production car trials, known by the initials PCT, are open to pretty much any two wheel drive production cars that do not have LSDs (limited slip differential). These are fairly common events, often run by local clubs, in sloping fields. A number of hills are set up and cars attempt them one after the other. PCTs are the domain of small, open, specialist cars such as the Marlin, but that's not to say that your everyday saloon car is no good; it is, but will likely run in a different class.

Sporting trials

Sporting trials are very similar to PCTs although the cars are different. Very different, in fact: I was alluding to the Marlin in my earlier reference to 'funny little cars', although I've since seen a sporting trials car. They are just plain weird. Skinny, front tyres steer with an astounding amount of lock, whilst the fatter driven rear wheels run with their tyres nearly flat to gain traction. Each wheel can be braked individually using a system of 'fiddle' brakes. The engines are never bigger than 1650cc and sit right up by the front wheels. And, of course, there are two seats, both of which are used.

Classic trials

Classic trials are almost a separate discipline but the principle behind them is the same as that of the sporting and production car variants: climbing big, muddy slopes.

Classic trials are not just for classic cars and many different and more modern cars compete. The only classic thing about classic trials is the format of the events; a classic trial is to a PCT what a multi-venue stage rally is to a single venue event.

Today's classic trials are an evolution of the reliability trials of the 1930s, where top manufacturers pitted their products against each other over long distances and steep, unsurfaced hills. A timing element is involved but only really to keep the event running on time and not as a competitive element. Most classic trials cover in the region of 70-100 miles on the public road between the so-called observed sections. The observed sections are, to all intents and purposes, individual hills from a sporting trial or a PCT and marked in the same way. There are usually around 16 of these observed sections. However, there are differences. Stop and restart tests are a fairly frequent challenge and involve bringing the car to a stop on a steep slope that is most likely covered in thick mud. That's the easy bit; you then have to get the thing going forward again with absolutely no backward movement. Speed tests usually settle a tie-break situation. Motor cycles often compete in classic

trials as well as cars and, in fact, bike clubs organise many events.

Three events that take place each year are the peak of all trialling events - the MCC (motor cycle club) classics. These three events have a road mileage of anything up to 450 miles. They start at midnight and finish at 5pm, and are, perhaps, the most gruelling of all amateur motorsports.

Because of the start time many of the observed sections are tackled in the dark. The marking system is different, too, with competitors either passing (cleaning) or failing a section. A 'gold' is the reward for cleaning all of the sections on an event. If a competitor manages to gain a gold in all three MCC classics in a season, he is awarded a 'triple' - the Holy Grail of trialling. The MCC classics have a history extending back to before the first world war.

BASIC EQUIPMENT

A two wheel drive car that meets the regulations.
Valid club membership card.
National B competition licence if required.
Someone to bounce for you.
For sporting trials, a sporting trials car.

PERSONAL EXPERIENCE

My first trial was of the production car variety and was a rather last-minute affair. A quick phone call to the organisers and I got myself a late entry for a slightly increased fee.

I made the short drive through the Downs to a muddy field on the outskirts of Dorking in Surrey. Now, I hadn't really done any research on the event or even, as it happened, the discipline, so knew it was going to be a fairly steep learning curve.

The car was given a quick once

over for scrutineering, and then I had to prove the old banger didn't have a limited slip diff by placing the right front wheel on a set of rollers and trying to pull away. I was one of the first to arrive and asked the clerk of the course to give me a few pointers; he was kind enough to show me all of the courses and how the numbers worked.

There were six hills that we would attempt twice each before lunch, and then a different six hills after we'd finished munching our burgers, again twice. More and more cars started to arrive, many of which bore stickers saying "MSA British Championship." The terrible truth dawned on me; this wasn't a small, clubman's event, oh no. this was National B level, and my first PCT was a round of the British Championship!

It wasn't just the learning curve that was steep, either; from the driving seat of my car, this particular section of the Surrey hills made Snowdon look like a gentle incline. As if that wasn't bad enough I had a complete stranger sitting next to me whose sole purpose was to jump up and down like a lunatic if it looked as if we were starting to lose traction. (The complete stranger in this case was a young guy who came along to watch and ended up bouncing for me and also another chap in a Peugeot.)

I pulled up to the first hill, and saw that getting past ten should be easy. Getting away from the start line took a lot of clutch control and the car crept past 12 with a lot of wheelspin and stopped. So, 11 points - not a great start.

The next hill started at the top of the first hill. Running along the crest, dipping up and down between trees, the surface was loose and dry but still fairly soft; this was going to be really tough. Just how tough I was about to find out. Most of the other cars had

And you thought finding a space in the company car park was difficult!

cleaned the hill and were waiting at the start. I, on the other hand, was on the foot of the hill. I tried to get up and got about halfway when the front wheels just dug in and spun till the tyres started smoking. I depressed the clutch pedal and rolled back down the hill. At the bottom I drove along the base of the bowl a bit, turned around and raced forward as fast as I could along the flatter section before turning into the hil. I got stuck ten meters or so short of the top.

As I rolled back to the bottom I caught an ominous whiff of hot clutch. Ignoring it I turned the car around and dived down the hill with the intention of going up the far side of the valley which was not as steep. Well, it wasn't a great idea and I failed again to reach the summit. I returned to the foot of the hill once more and paused. The young chap who was bouncing for me came over from the Peugeot, in which he was also bouncing, with a message from the driver of the French car. Breathlessly he said: "Do it in reverse." I tried it and it worked a treat. I got to the 9 board on the hill and would have gone further but the car understeered on a tight turn and bumped into the 8 board. I was getting better but the clutch was getting worse. A couple of hills later with some more advice and I was going a bit better.

You know how you see four wheel drives trundling along the middle lane of the M25 without a speck of mud on them? I bet the drivers of those wonder why they see two wheel drive 'rep mobiles' covered in the stuff - this is why!

On the fifth hill I thought I was on the way to my first clean of the day. The hill started at the bottom of the bowl on the edge of a small wood, and ran fairly straight along the flat through some very soft, broken up soil to point 9, where the course looped round between two trees and wriggled its way up through the woods to an unseen summit.

Waiting on the start line and trying not to spend too much time eyeing up the girl, I looked down the route and tried to work out the best way through the soft mud. Something caught my eye through the trees; a mangled, burnt out and quite dead Mini. Good omen ... I had decided before I saw the ex-Mini that the best way to tackle this section was to use

my favourite technique - the bull in the china shop: flat-out to the trees, using the momentum to skim across the mud and the handbrake to get around the first turn. I went for it.

Unfortunately. it worked a bit too well. I was straight off the line, spreading topsoil over the rest of the cars waiting to start, an unhealthy dose of wheelspin accompanying a strong whiff of burning clutch. We leapt off the line and hurtled towards the first turn, which was at the 8 point board. My attempts to turn the car on the soft soil into the first, square, right hand bend resulted in the car pointing directly at a big tree. I was left with a dilemma at speed: should I try and keep going around the corner in a car with terrible understeer, and a solid-looking oak in my path, or should I bottle it, tug the steering left and abandon the run? No contest, really; I didn't want my car to end up like the Mini …

The loose soil had taken its toll on the old car, and on the drive up to the next hill the clutch got far too hot; a nasty-smelling cloud of smoke billowed from the engine bay. I jumped out and opened the bonnet; smoke poured out of the transmission casing and the clutch was on fire, just a little. It was the end of my event as a competitor. I waited by the car with an extinguisher for about fifteen minutes in case it got worse, but it didn't.

I spent the rest of the day marshalling, and realised what a great spectator event this is. If you have to marshal just one event I would recommend a round of the British production car trial championship.

By the way, no-one cleaned every hill though on some of the later hills the local drivers in the clubman's class did better than the British championship crews! Trials are not always this difficult, and my car had a bad clutch which had already failed on a few rallies and should have been replaced earlier.

Trials advice

"Lower your car's tyre pressures as this will give the car a bigger footprint and better traction in the mud."

"If your car has a dodgy clutch don't compete."

"Bring a larger proportioned friend along to 'bounce' for you."

"If you start to lose traction and get stuck with your wheels spinning, try turning from lock-to-lock: the tyres may well find some grip."

"There are two ways to clean a hill, trickling or blasting."

"Ask experienced competitors how to drive the specialist cars."

"Before attempting a hill, walk it with your bouncer, so you know where it goes."

Chapter 14
What car?

Standard production cars can be huge fun with the right (or possibly wrong!) approach. (Courtesy Colin Shipway)

Almost any standard road car will make a most competitive competition car, and often modification is not necessary. Some cars, however, are more popular than others, and if you don't already have a car to campaign, you should seriously consider the following.

The Peugeot 205 is one of - if not the - most popular competition car in the UK, as it excels in all disciplines. It even has its own hugely successful stage rally series. The French-made car handles very well, with a slight tendency to oversteer. The two GTi versions (1.6 and 1.9) are fairly powerful. Parts are freely and cheaply available, and the car is easy to maintain. It could be said, though, that the model's engineering is not as solid as it could be.

If the Peugeot is not *the* most popular competition car then the Mini certainly is. Alec Issigonis probably didn't envisage it when he designed his masterpiece, but the car has been the lynchpin of club motorsport for over 30 years. Kart-like handling has allowed it to carve its own little niche, and every discipline has a class for the little machine. Parts are not that hard to come by, and many specialist companies offer competition parts for reasonable prices. However, the safety standard of these old cars is not up to that of some of its more modern rivals. BMW's new version is becoming a potential clubman's staple, with a challenge race and hillclimb series, although only time will tell whether that is the case.

Rear wheel drive Ford Escorts are fairly commonplace on the rallying scene, but may lack the versatility of some shorter rivals. Competition parts are amongst the easiest to come by.

The Escort's little brother, the Fiesta, is part of the scenery on the circuit racing scene.

More expensive but certainly more fun, and highly versatile, are the Lotus 7 derivatives Caterham, Westfield and Locost, although, being open, not recommended for rallying. The circuit driving scene is awash with the lightweight cars, many of which are homemade.

My personal favourite is the MkII Volkswagen Golf, a fairly unorthodox choice but, I feel, a good one. The rock-solid construction of the German car allows it to take some serious punishment will very little resultant unreliability. Powerful versions such as the famous GTi and Supercharged G60 can pose a real threat in competition. Parts are dirt cheap and the car is, in essence, very simple - and therefore easy - to maintain. Competition parts are available but not as readily as those for some other cars. The Golf's biggest shortfalls are weight and built-in understeer, both of which can be remedied fairly easily.

The most famous of all the clubman's cars is the old Mini, which has aged well. It's rare for an event not to include at least one. It is almost made for autotesting, is ever-present on stage rallies, has its own class in autocross, and a number of highly successful circuit racing series. It's also heap to buy and every single nuance is well known. There are also a number of Mini-based cars such as the GTM and Mini Marcos.

CARS THE AUTHOR'S GONE CLUBBING WITH

1985 Volkswagen Golf CL
I bought my first car for just over £600, a somewhat tatty example of the massively under-powered 1275cc MkII. I competed just once with this car on a local Scatter rally and finished last. It did, however, transport me around the race circuits reliably until it

It is essential to use quality products on your competition car,
(Courtesy Colin Shipway)

was written off in an accident.

1985 (rebuilt 2000) Ford Fiesta XR2
I made my racing debut in the second East Surrey College racing Fiesta at Lydden Hill, finishing second in class at the end of the event. The fully race prepared car was sold and, as far as I know, still races.

1986 Volkswagen Golf GL
I bought another Golf to replace the first one, as I was impressed with how solid and corrosion-resistant the German cars were. This time I bought a more powerful (but still nothing special) 1595cc example for £450. I have used the car every day to the date of writing, and also used it to compete in almost every discipline in this book. The car has no modifications that cost more than £30 and has nothing that is not absolutely necessary. Simply fitting a good quality pair of tyres to the driven wheels cured the bad understeer that is common on all Golfs. The extra grip and improved handling given by these tyres, and a well looked after engine allied to the reliability of the German running gear, has made the Golf a strong road rally car.

TRACK DAYS

Track days have really blossomed in

A Brands Hatch winner (Courtesy Uniroyal Team Challenge)

popularity in the last few years. A track day, strictly speaking, isn't sport as there's no competitive element. Drivers bring along their cars and simply lap the circuit all day, usually overtaking on the left when a slower car is encountered.

The cars vary from everyday saloons to real auto-exotica manufactured by Ferrari, Porsche and TVR. The scene has boomed so much that the British sports car cottage industry is making cars designed specifically for track days. Recent offerings from Westfield and Radical looked like scaled-down Le Mans sports prototype racers.

Some track day organisers allow cars out on the track for unlimited amounts of time, an open pit lane. Some organisers run cars in batches according to car speed and/or driver ability. No licences are needed apart from an regular driving licence.

On a track day I took part in the cars ranged from a nearly unique Dare (no, I hadn't heard of it either) to a mini cab complete with taxi licence plate on the rear bumper. I was driving one of East Surrey College's racing Fords and the venue was a soaking wet airfield at Wethersfield in Essex. I got chatting to a number of other drivers and hitched a ride in the Dare (mad), a Caterham (windy) and a Lotus Elise (perfect!).

Track days are generally held on established motor racing circuits, but are also held at venues such as airfields. Track days are popular because of the relatively low cost of taking part and the amount of track time that is allowed. It's a good way to learn about driving at speed on a circuit and often there are instructors on hand to give free tuition on the correct techniques of driving.

However, track days do lack that important element, competition. Generally, cars are not timed, either, so you don't even have yourself to beat. Just flicking through the pages of *Circuit Driver* magazine will give an idea of just how huge track days have become. Is it sport? No, but it is fun motoring.

Rallying is both a summer and winter sport (Courtesy Andy Manston)

Glossary of terms

Motorsport has its own jargon and terminology, some of which you will probably already be familiar with, but some you may not.

ARDS	Association of Racing Driver Schools
ARKS	Association of Race karting Schools
ASN	A nation's governing body
BARS	British Association of Rally Schools
Blue Book	The MSA competitors' yearbook, an essential tome that contains all of the rules and regulations of UK motorsport.
BTD	Best Time of Day
Cleaning	A trials term meaning a perfect section result
Clubcross	A lesser version of Autocross
Colway	English rally tyre manufacturer
Compound	The hardness or softness of the tyre type
Cut-off switch	A single switch that shuts off all systems on the car, often marked by a lightning bolt
Endurance racing	Long distance events such as the Le Mans 24 hours race.
FIA	Federation Internationale De L'Automobile - The world governing body
Four wheel drift	The art of making a car corner on the limit (see moment!)
FTD	Fastest Time of Day
Fuel cell	Safety fuel tank with an Aramid bag inside a metal case
GRs	General Regulations
Intermediate	A tyre in-between a full wet and a slick, superb for improving grip on road-going cars
Knobblies	Special off-road tyre.
Moment	When an accident or spin is narrowly averted, it's known as this

MSA	Motor Sports Association: the UK governing body
Nomex	Flame-proof material that most race wear is made from
Pace notes	Used by rally navigators to read the road ahead and pass the information to the driver
Proban	A flame-retardant material that some overalls are made from
Progressive springs	Suspension part that becomes progressively stiffer under cornering
Race control	The office where all administration takes place
Red book	The MSA officials' yearbook
Regs	Specific regulations for an event, these are sent to competitors about a month beforehand and contain the offical entry form
Ride height	The level at which a car sits above the road
Roll	See spin, but generally more serious
Rollcage (also rollbar and roll hoop)	A cage-like structure to protect occupants in the event of a rollover
Scrutineering	All cars entered in an event must have a safety and eligibility check before being allowed to compete, which is known as scrutineering
Shunt	Crash
Signatures	Proof of completion of an event indicated on the reverse of a competition licence
Signing on	A competitor's paperwork is checked prior to the start of an event, so named because the competitor signs the indemnity forms
Slicks	Special dry weather racing tyres that have no tread to increase surface area and therefore grip; much softer than road tyres and far more expensive
Special stage (ss)	A competitive section of a rally
Specials	Unique one-off, generally homemade, purpose-built competition cars
Spin	When the tyres lose grip and the car rotates
SRs	Supplementary Regulations
Timing strut	A flat section of flat material that is attached to the front of the car which breaks a timing beam. Used only in speed events.
Transponder	A microchip installed in some club racing series and nearly all karts, used for timing
Wets	Wet weather tyres with tread to disperse water. Mostly standard road tyres
Wing	An aerofoil used to generate negative lift or downforce
WRC	World Rally Championship

How To Power Tune The BMC/BL/Rover 998cc A-Series Engine
Des Hammill

The 998 A-Series powers Minis and Metros in particular. The book's advice can also be used to uprate Midget/Sprite 948cc units to high performance 998cc units. A complete guide to obtaining maximum power with reliability from the 998cc version of this engine.

How to Choose Camshafts & Time Them for Maximum Power
Des Hammill

How to choose the right camshaft or camshafts for YOUR individual application. Takes the mystery out of camshaft timing and tells you how to find optimum timing for maximum power. Applies to *all* four stroke car-type engines.

How to Build & Power Tune Holley Carburetors
Des Hammill

The complete guide to choosing and specifying Holley carbs for road or track performance. Uniquely, this book allows the identification of secondhand carbs and individual components, including all metering blocks, so you can buy and build with confidence.

How to Power Tune Ford SOHC 4-cylinder 'Pinto' & Cosworth DOHC Engines
Updated New Edition!
Des Hammill

Build a reliable high-performance 1600/1800/2000 'Pinto' engine for road or track, using many stock parts and without wasting money. Covers Cosworth versions of Pinto engines, too, and fitting Cosworth heads to Pinto blocks.

How to Power Tune The BMC/BL/Rover 1275cc A-Series Engine
Des Hammill

A complete guide to modifying the 1275cc A-Series engine for high-performance with reliability. Maximum use of original equipment components. The A-Series engine was used in many Austin/Morris/Rover models including Minis, Metros, 1300s, Allegros, MG Midgets, A-H Sprites, Maestros, Marinas, etc.

How to Build, Modify & Power Tune Cylinder Heads New Edition!
Peter Burgess & David Gollan

The complete practical guide to successfully modifying cylinder heads for maximum power, economy and reliability. Avoids wasting money on modifications that don't work. Applies to almost every car/motorcycle (does not apply to 2-stroke engines).

How to Build & Power Tune Distributor-type Ignition Systems
Des Hammill

How to build an excellent ignition system and how to optimise the ignition timing of any high-performance engine. Applies to four-stroke engines with distributor-type ignition systems (including electronic ignition modules). Does not cover engines controlled by ECUs (engine control units).

How to Build & Power Tune Ford V8 221, 255, 260, 289, 302 & 351cu in smallblock engines
Des Hammill

The complete guide to building a powerful and reliable high performance Ford V8 smallblock for street or track. Covers limitations of standard parts, component mods, component interchanges, blueprinting and professional build tips.

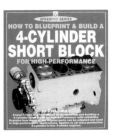

How to Blueprint & Build a 4-Cylinder Short Block for High Performance
Des Hammill

How to blueprint *any* 4-cylinder, four-stroke engine's short block to obtain maximum performance and reliability without wasting money. Choosing components, crank & con-rod bearings, cylinder block, con-rods, pistons, camshaft, balancing, expert check-build procedures and much more.

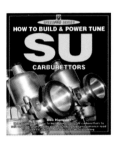

How to Build & Power Tune SU Carburettors
Des Hammill

Did you know that SUs can give almost as much performance as Webers & Dellortos? Here's an expert guide to building and modifying SU carburettors to suit high performance applications. Includes reprofiling needles & how to 'jet' SUs for almost any application.

How to Build Your Own Tiger Avon Sports Car for Road or Track
Jim Dudley

Step-by-step guide to building your dream Sportscar on a budget. The Avon is based on readily available Ford Sierra mechanical components: you can use a straight 4 or V8 engine of your choice, including Pinto, Zetec or Rover K-Series. All components, including used parts available from Tiger Sportscars

How to Blueprint & Build a V8 Short Block for High Performance
Des Hammill

Expert practical advice from an experienced race engine builder on how to build a V8 short block engine for high performance use, using mainly stock parts - including crankshaft and rods. Applies to all sizes and makes of V8 engine with overhead valves operated by pushrods.

How to Power Tune Rover V8 Engines for Road & Track
Des Hammill

Maximum performance & reliability for minimum money from 3.5, 3.9, 4.0 & 4.6-litre engines (1967 to date). Includes limitations of standard components; short block preparation/clearances; solving oiling & main cap problems of pre-'94 blocks; full details of head modifications; and much more.

How to Build & Modify Sportscar & Kitcar Suspension & Brakes
Enlarged New Edition!
Des Hammill

Get the best handling and braking from sportscars/kitcars with wishbone front suspension, coil springs and telescopic shockers. Includes 'chassis' integrity, suspension geometry, ride height, camber, castor, kpi, springs, shock absorbers, testing and adjustment.

How to Modify Volkswagen Beetle Suspension, Brakes and Chassis for High Performance
James Hale

How to get the best handling and braking from your Volkswagen Beetle. Covers front & rear suspension, 'chassis' integrity, suspension geometry, ride height, camber, castor, kpi, springs, shock absorbers, testing and adjustment. (Not 1302 &1303 models).

How to Build & Power Tune Weber & Dellorto DCOE & DHLA Carburetors -
New 3rd Edition!
Des Hammill

All you could want to know about the world's most famous and popular high-performance sidedraught carburetors. Strip and rebuild. Tuning. Jetting. Choke sizes. Application formulae gives the right set-up for *your* car. Covers all Weber DCOE & Dellorto DHLA carburetors.

Index

750 MC 57

ACGBI 10
ACSMC 10, 25
Alfa Romeo 25, 28
Anderson, Colin 23
ARDS 11, 60
ASEMC 10
ASWMC 25

BARC 57
Bosher - Jones, David 39
Bournemouth MC 28
Brands Hatch 9, 37, 48, 69
Brooklands 9, 54, 55, 57, 98, 101
Brookes (Oxford / Formula) 107, 110, 111
Buckmore Park, 41, 42
BRSCC 10, 57, 60, 63, 66. 69

Castle Combe 12
CUAC 108
Central Sussex MC 27
'Chin' 74
Club 100 41
Crystal Palace 8, 55, 56, 101
Dawson, Mark 78
Donington Park 55, 56, 101

East Surrey College 62, 65
Escort 26, 29, 63, 75, 76

Extinguishers 14, 22

Ferrari 9, 96
FIA 10, 14

Go - Kart 39
Goodwood 56

Hall, Daren 78
Hilton, Peter 39
Hopkirk, Paddy 34, 71
Howell, Martin 41

Ingels, Art 38, 39, 42
IUKC 108

Jacobs, Dave 79

Kemsley, Jack 72

Lancia 28, 29, 76
Locke - King, Hugh 54
Longcross 48, 78
Lotus 8
Luckings, Terry 79
Lydden Hill 9, 56, 62, 63

Mason, Chris 41
McRae Alister 71
McRae, Colin 33, 71
Metro 6R4 8

Middlesex AC 98
MSA, 10, 11, 14, 26, 34, 49, 50, 62, 65,78, 112, 116

North, Fat Oliver 88
NUMC 108

Oxford MC 33
OUMDC 108

Rally of Kent 50, 76
Rochester MC, 104
Rockingham 57
Roll Cage 16, 67
Rye House 41

Sand - o - cross 24
SEMSEC 57, 104
Sevenoaks & District Motor Club 8, 35, 36, 37, 50, 72, 74, 78
Senna, Ayrton 9, 43, 60
Silverstone 9, 56
Smith, Richard 9
Solo 2 23

Taunton MC 24
Tulips 87

Ulster Rally 34

Wheatcroft, Tom 56